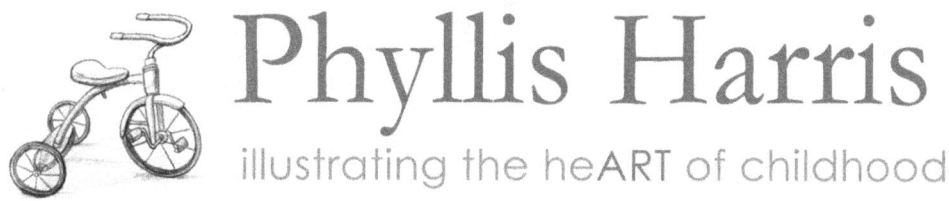

Phyllis Harris
illustrating the heART of childhood

Hello friends!

I am so honored that you chose this coloring book to enjoy.

You may want to try using crayons, colored pencils, or even pastels in your color book. The possibilities are endless. If using markers, I recommend using a piece of card stock to help ensure that there will be no bleed-through.

Coloring is intended to be relaxing so don't worry about perfection. Have fun, enjoy and slip back to that time of wonder in childhood when you colored for the pure joy of it.

Please share your colored creations with me over at Facebook or Instagram,
Facebook: http://www.facebook.com/PhyllisHarrisDesigns
Instagram: https://instagram.com/phyllisharrisdesigns

To see more of my art be sure to visit phyllisharrisdesigns.com.

Wishing you many blessings,

Make a *wish*...
Anything is possible.

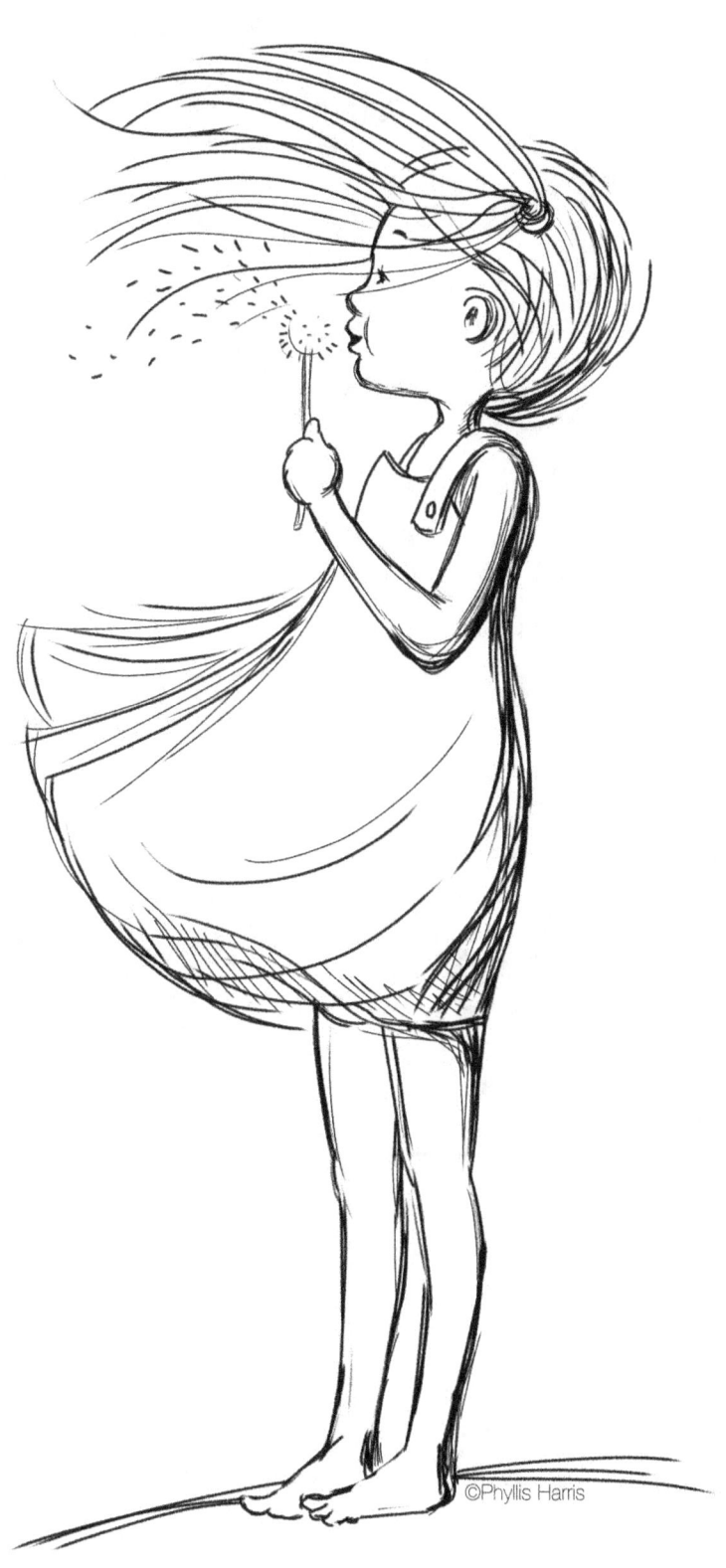

©Phyllis Harris

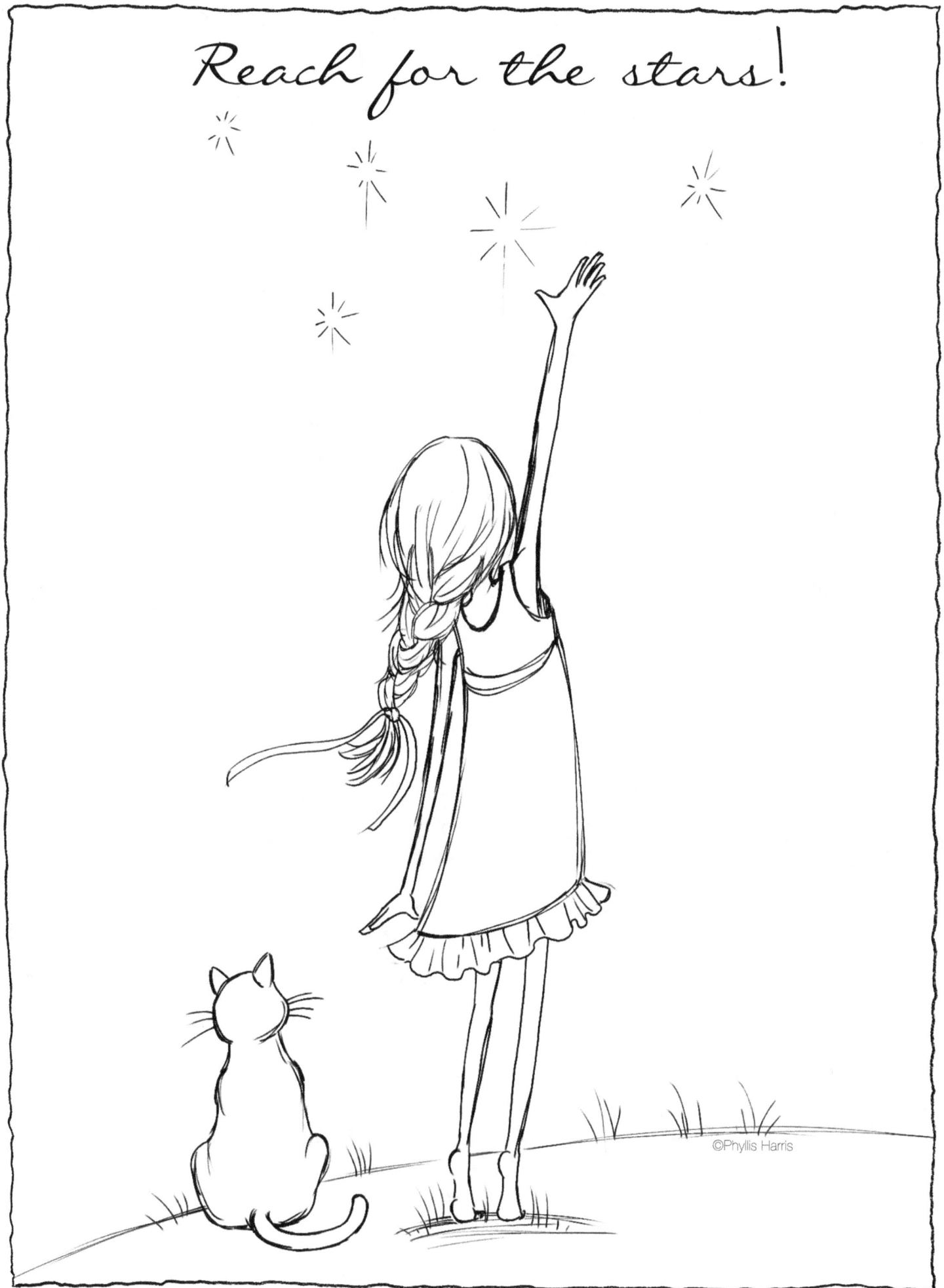

The *wind* on my face
    is the whisper of *God*.

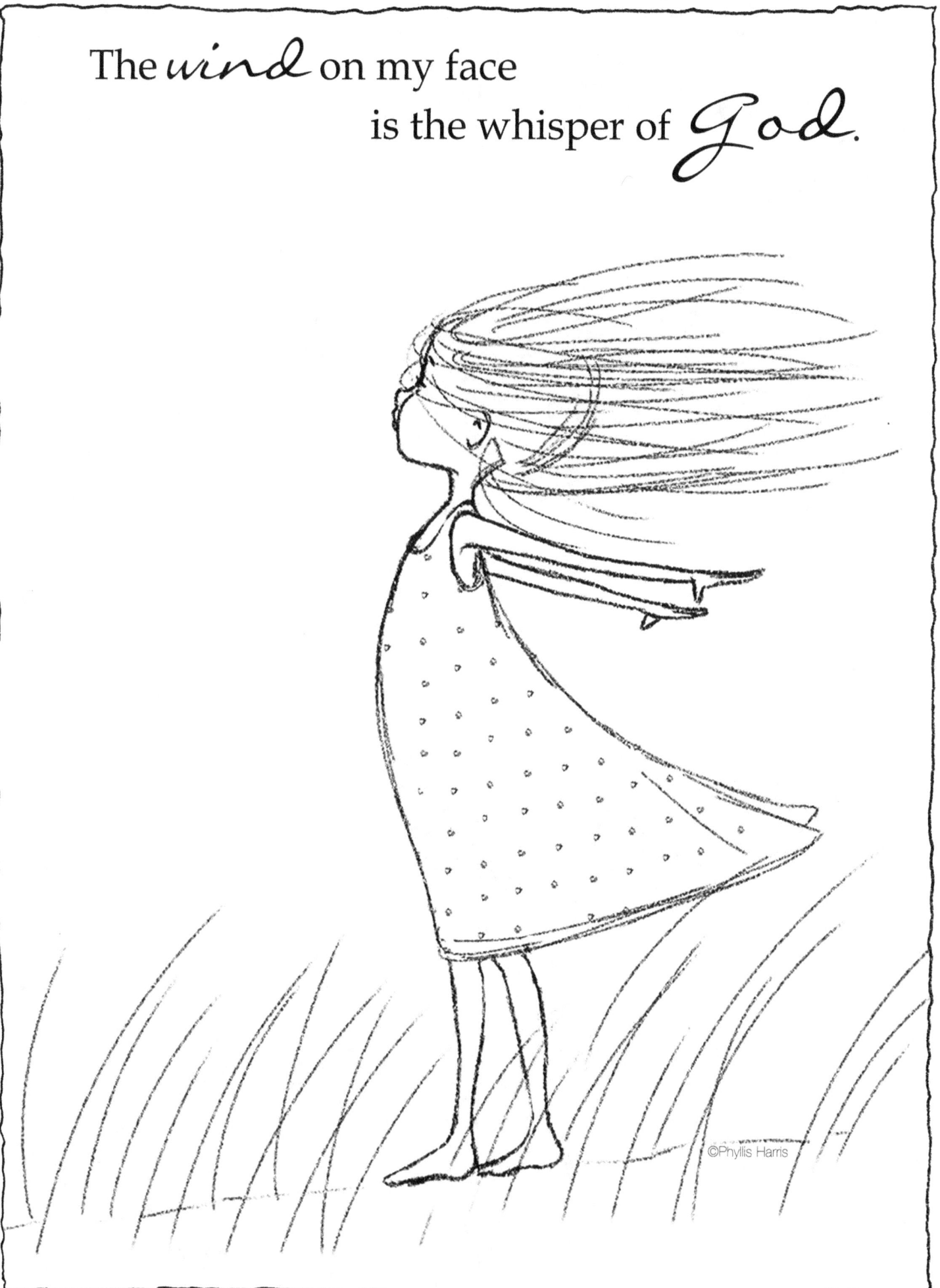

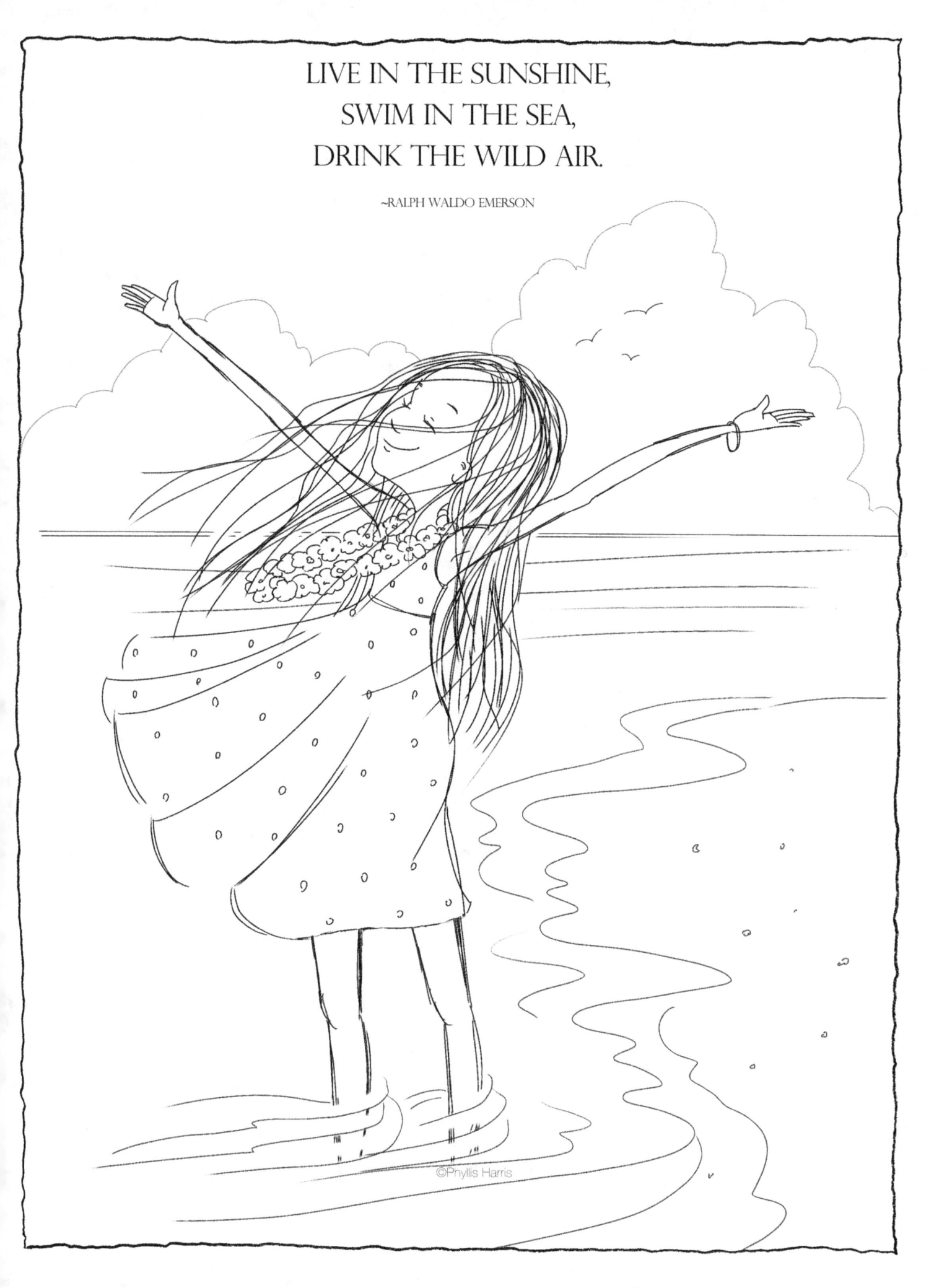

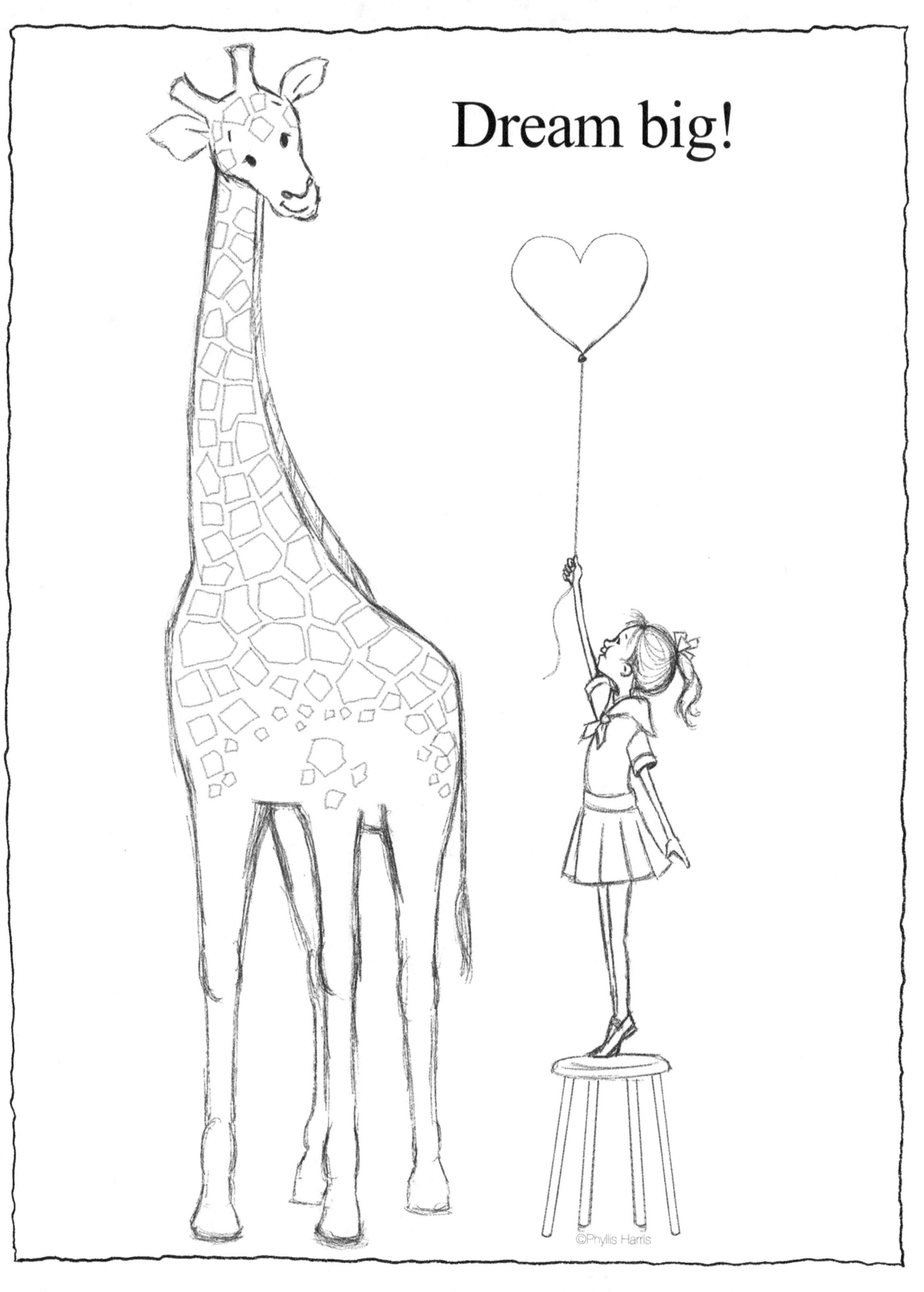

Dream big!

©Phyllis Harris

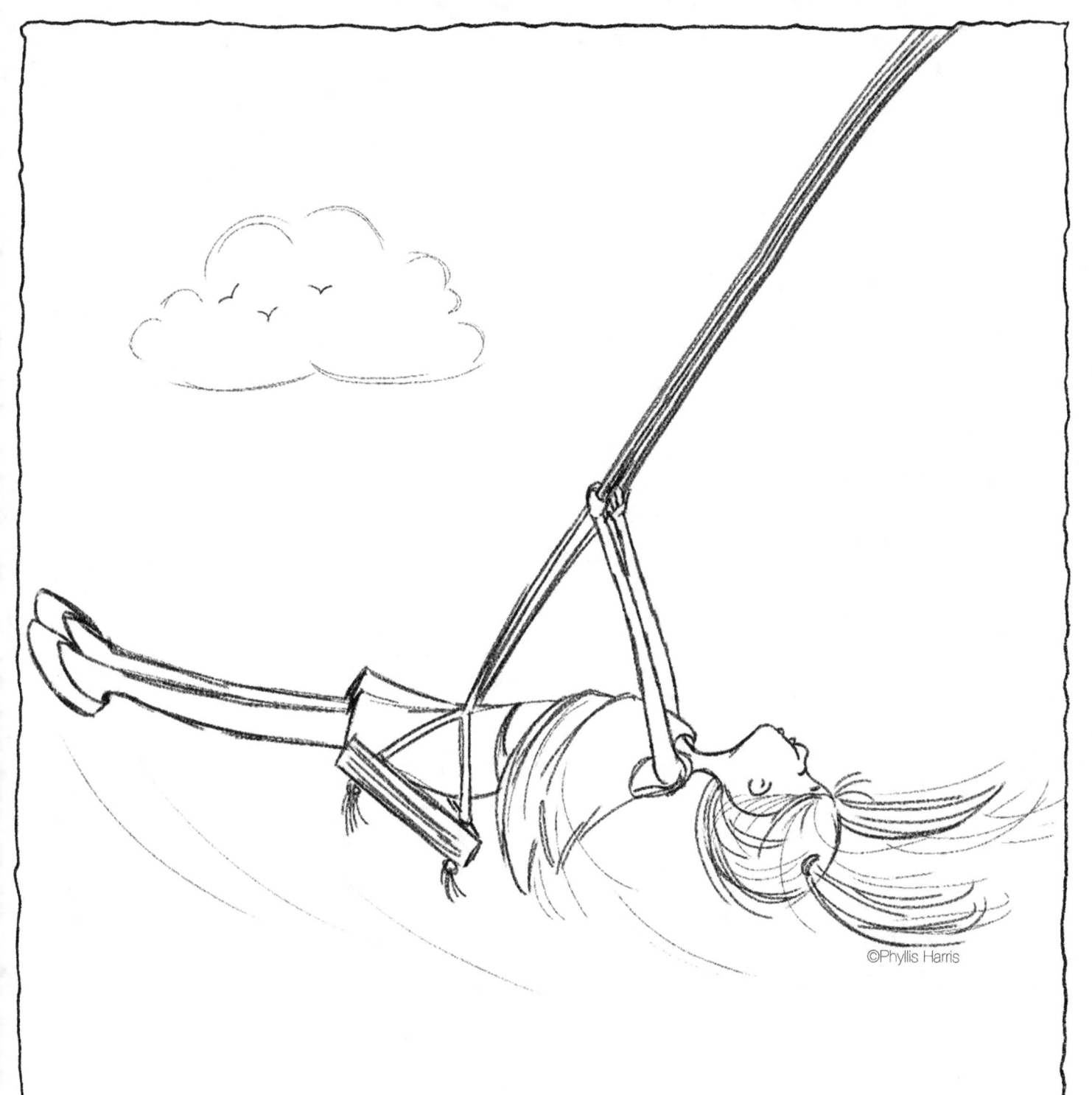

Let your imagination soar!

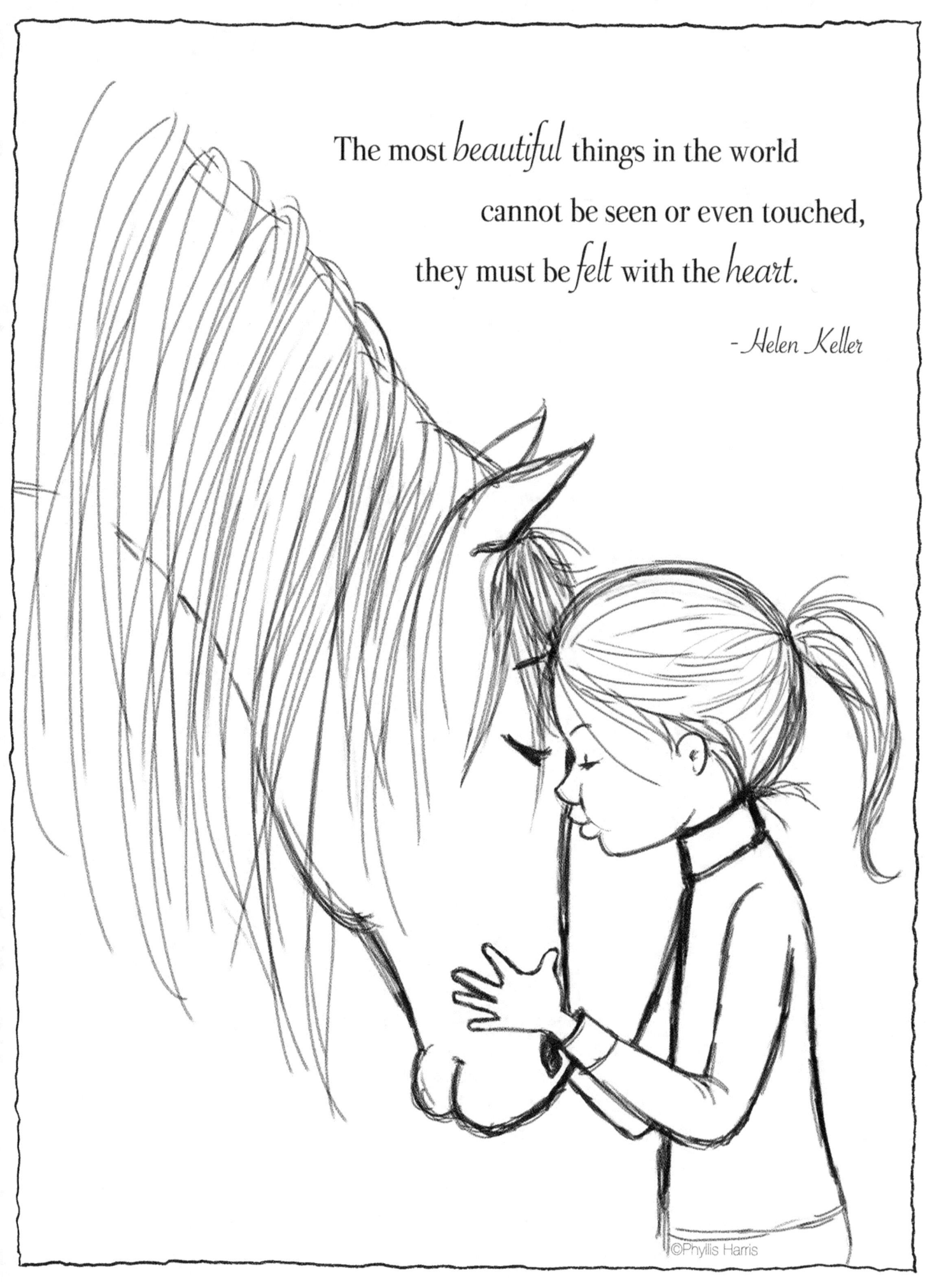

The most *beautiful* things in the world cannot be seen or even touched, they must be *felt* with the *heart.*

- Helen Keller

All I have seen teaches me to trust the creator

for all I have not seen.

-Ralph Waldo Emerson

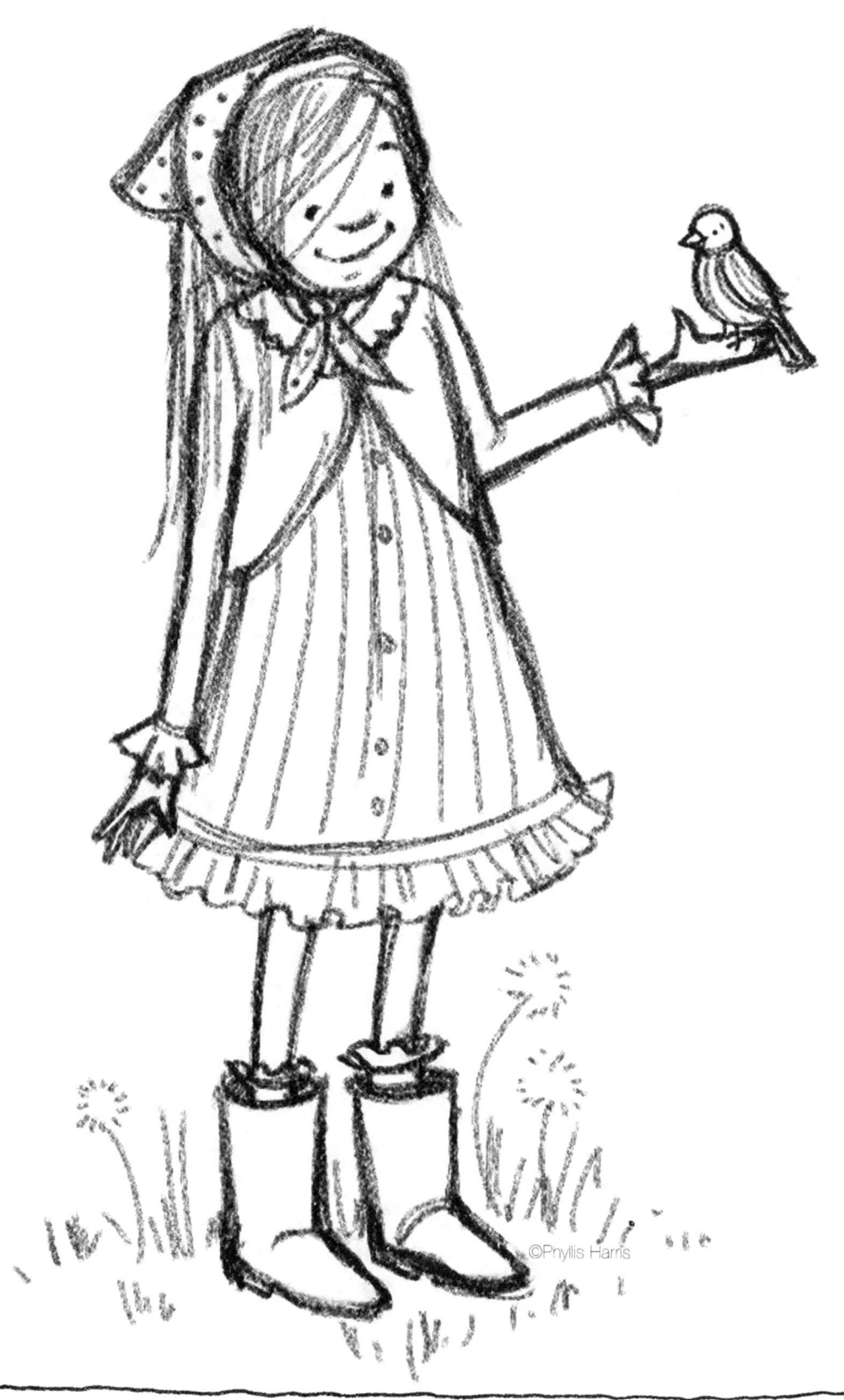

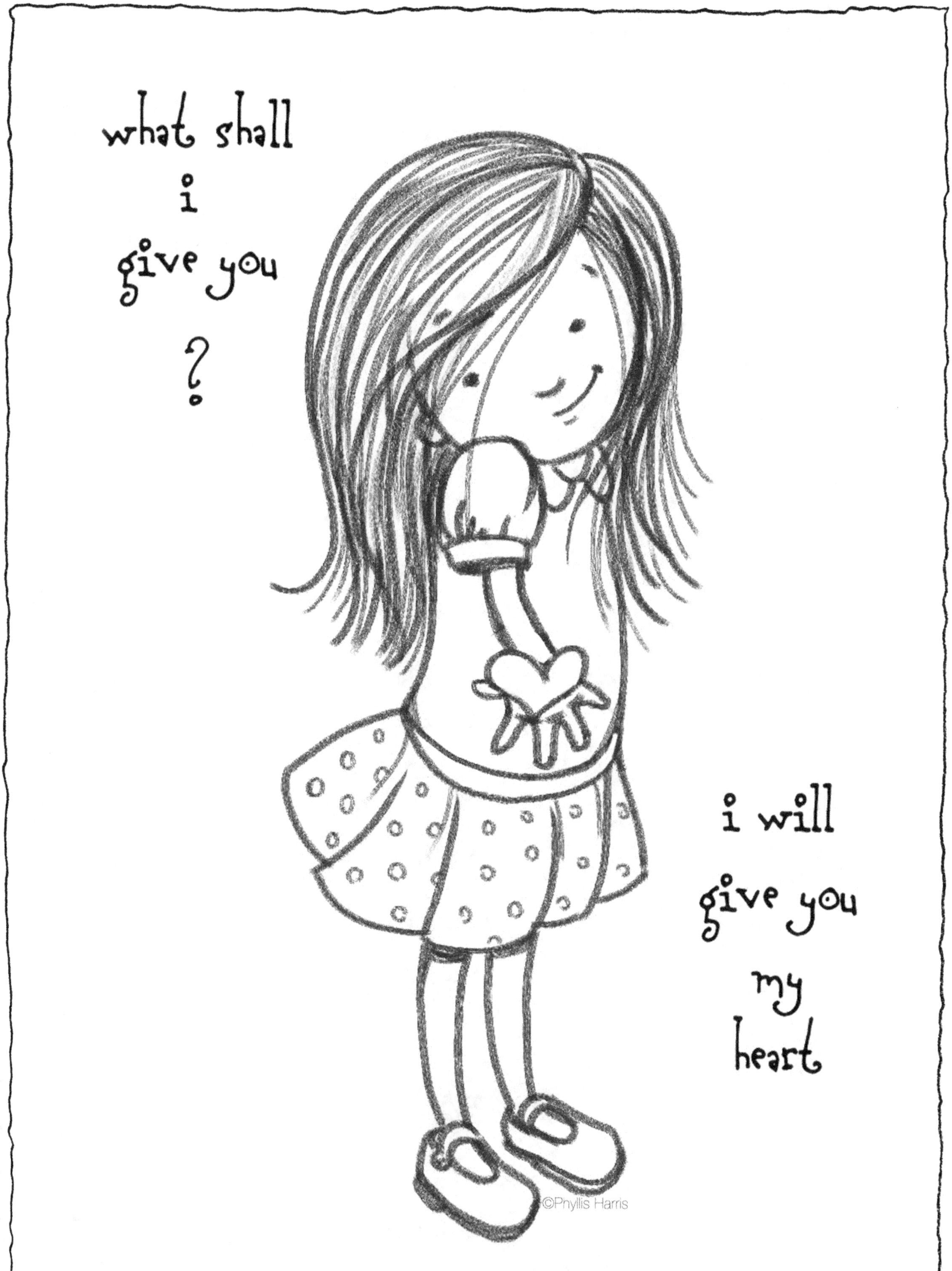
what shall
i
give you
?
i will
give you
my
heart
©Phyllis Harris

The most beautiful world
is always entered
through imagination.

~ Helen Keller

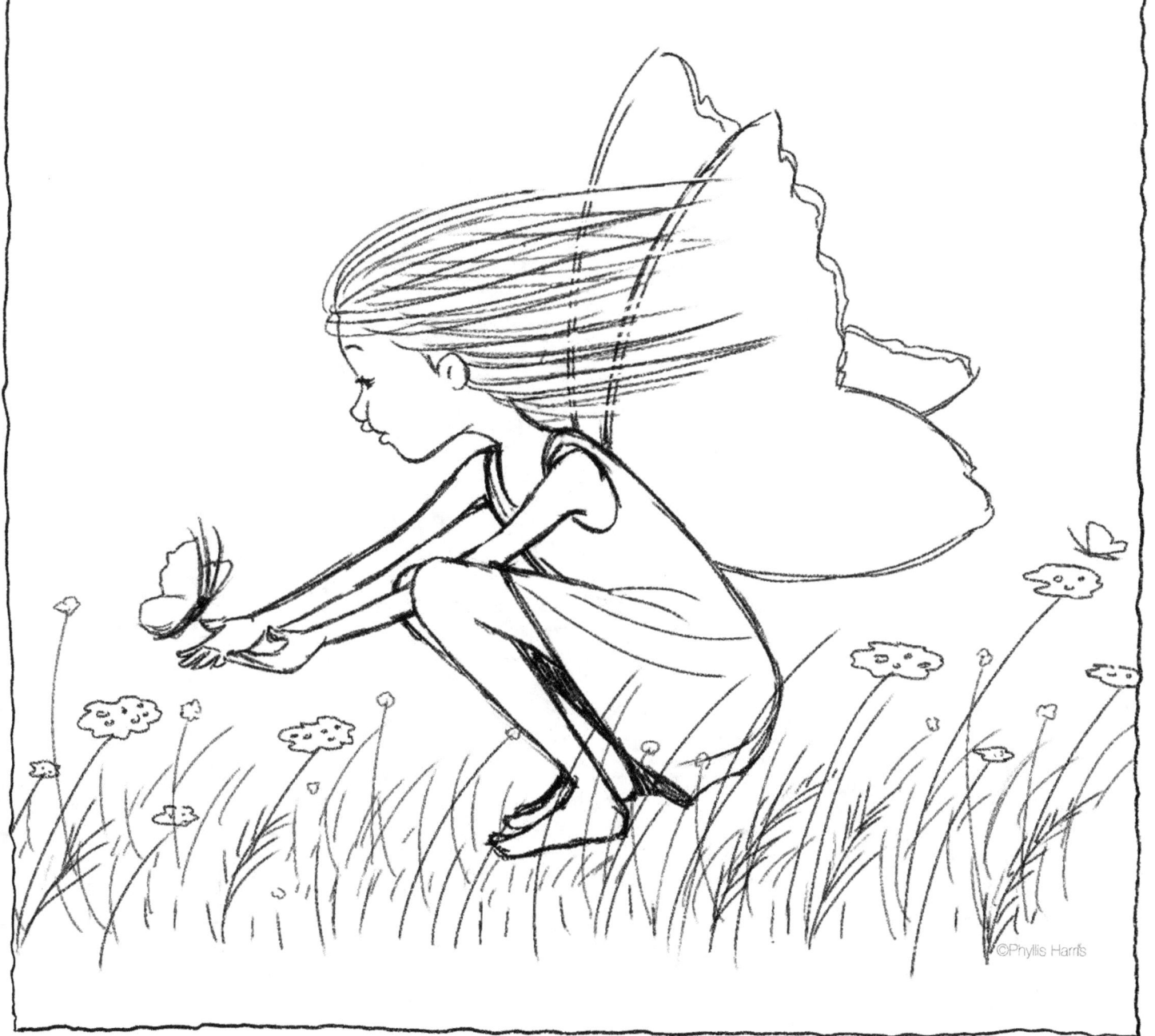

Sometimes,
we just need someone
to be there.

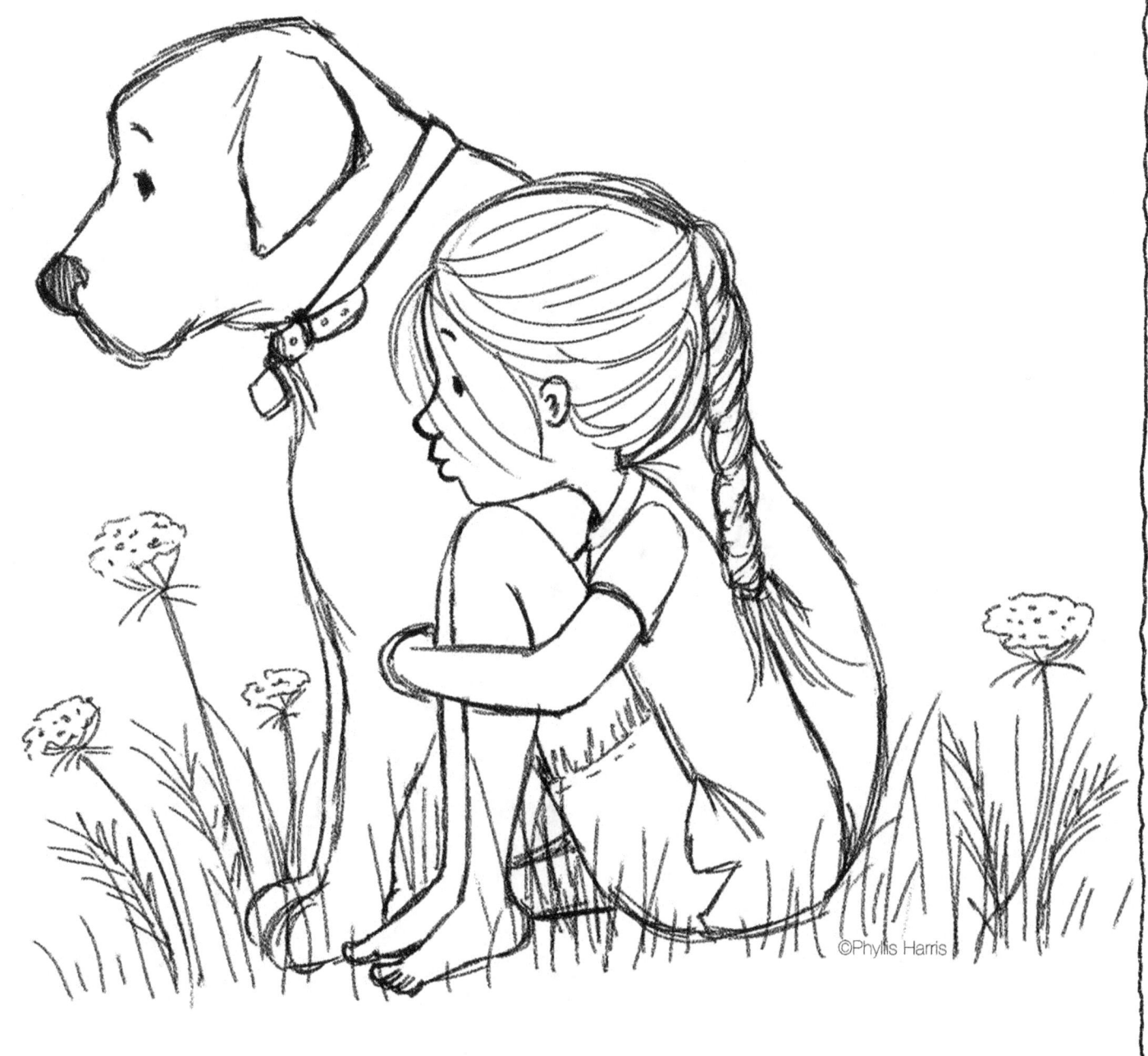

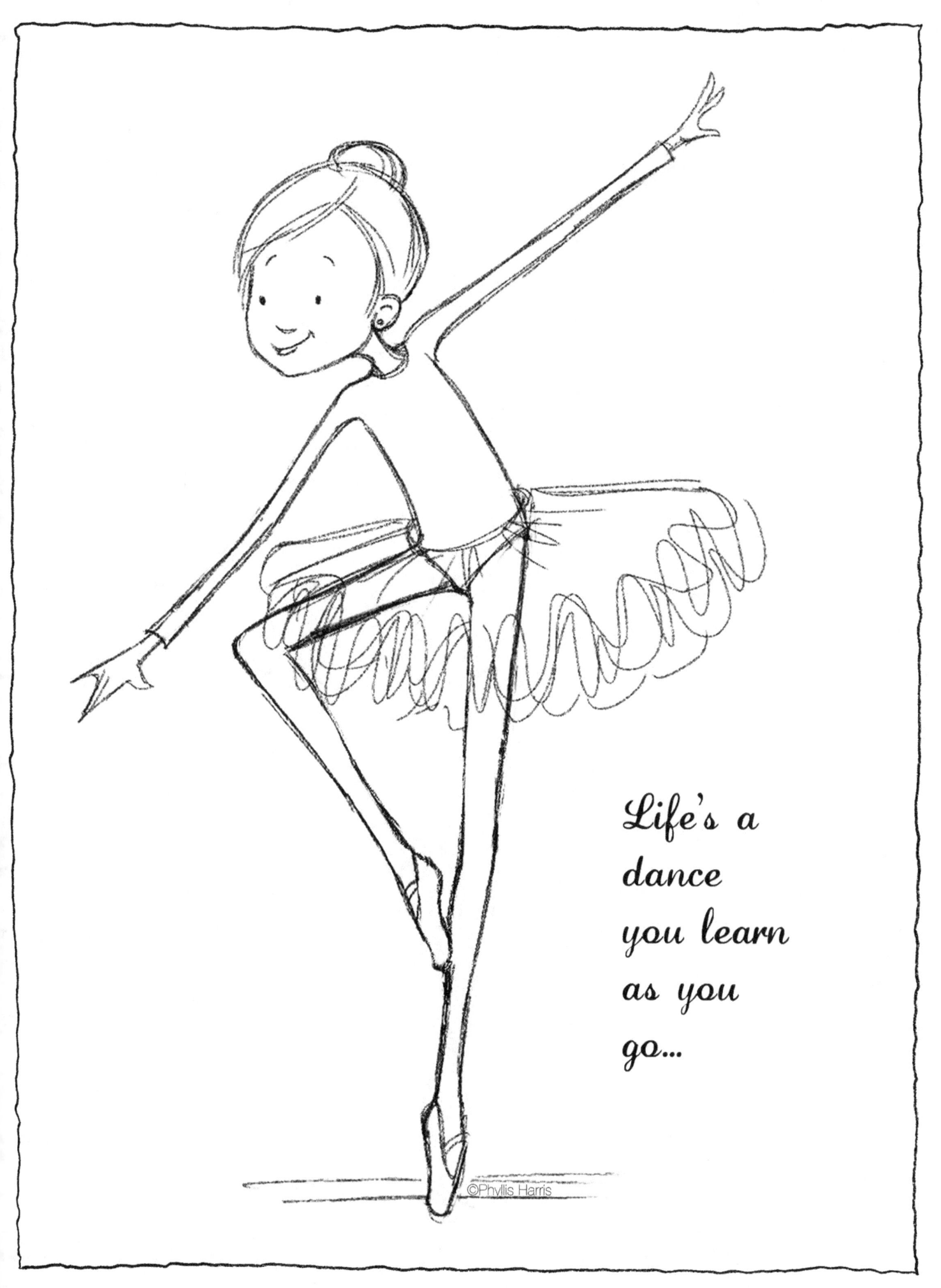

Life's a
dance
you learn
as you
go...

©Phyllis Harris

Blessed are the meek,
for they will inherit *the earth.*

Matthew 5:5

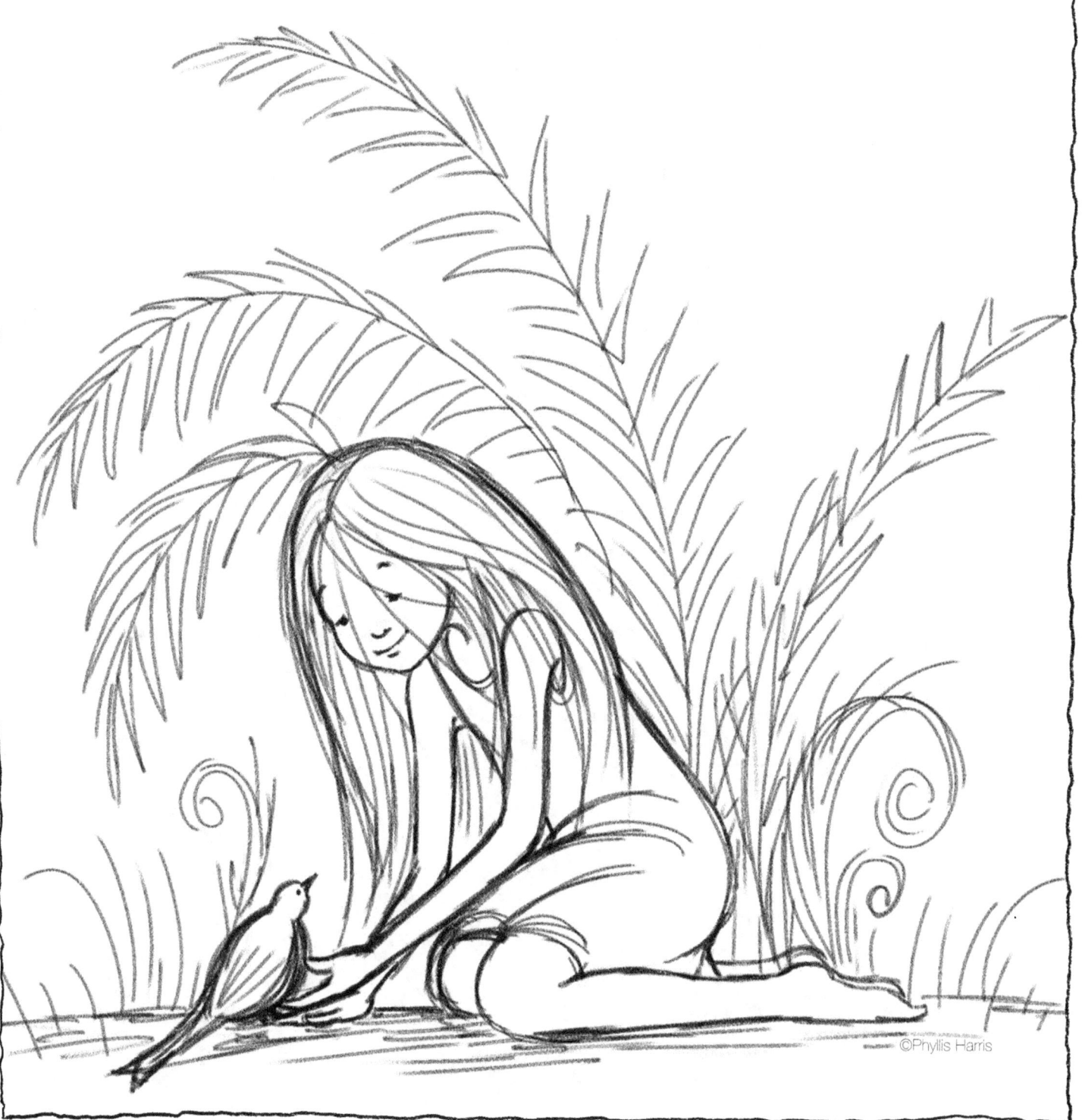

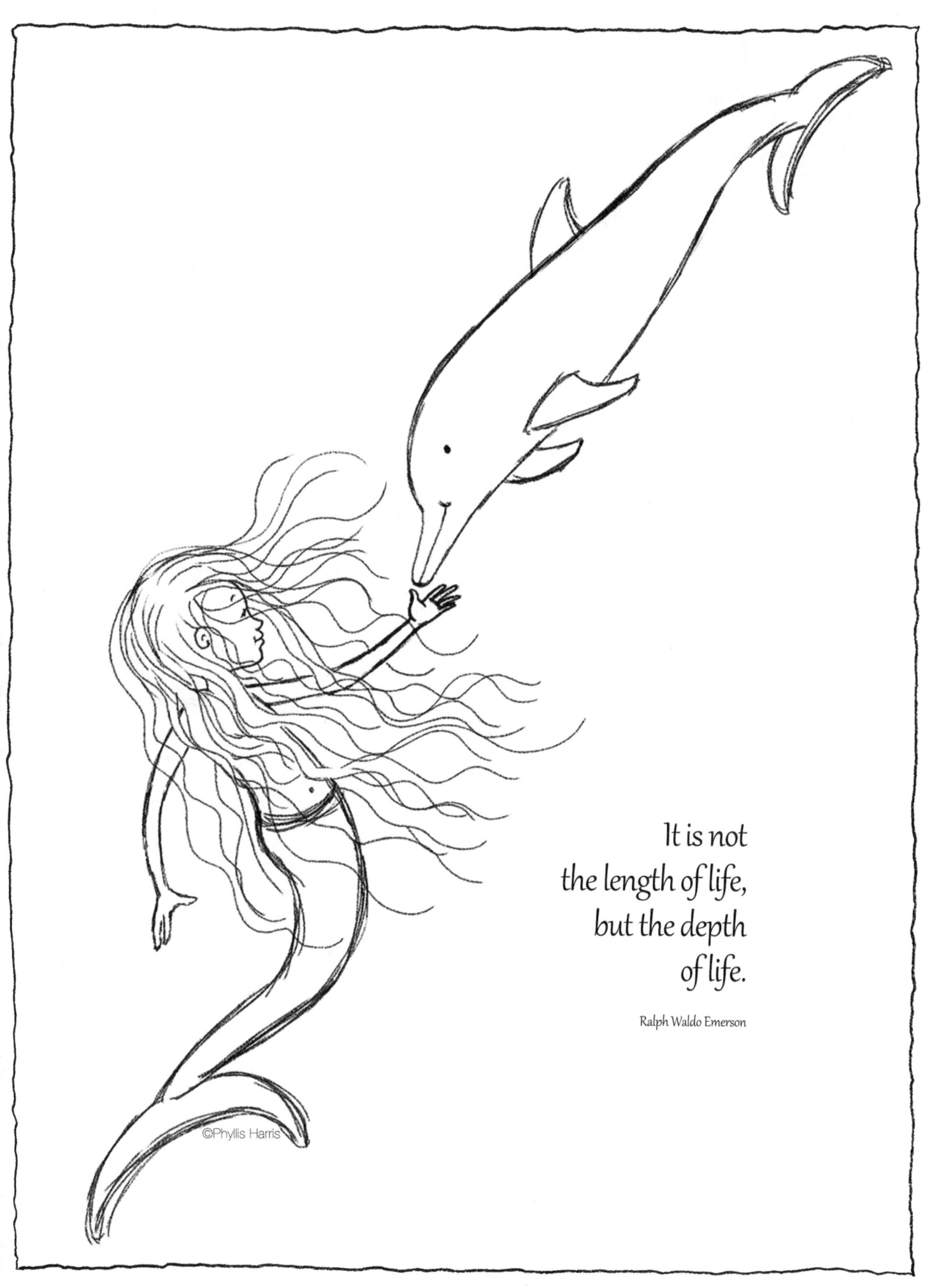

It is not
the length of life,
but the depth
of life.

Ralph Waldo Emerson

©Phyllis Harris

Let the fields be jubilant, and everything in them;
let all the trees of the forest sing for joy.

Psalm 96:12

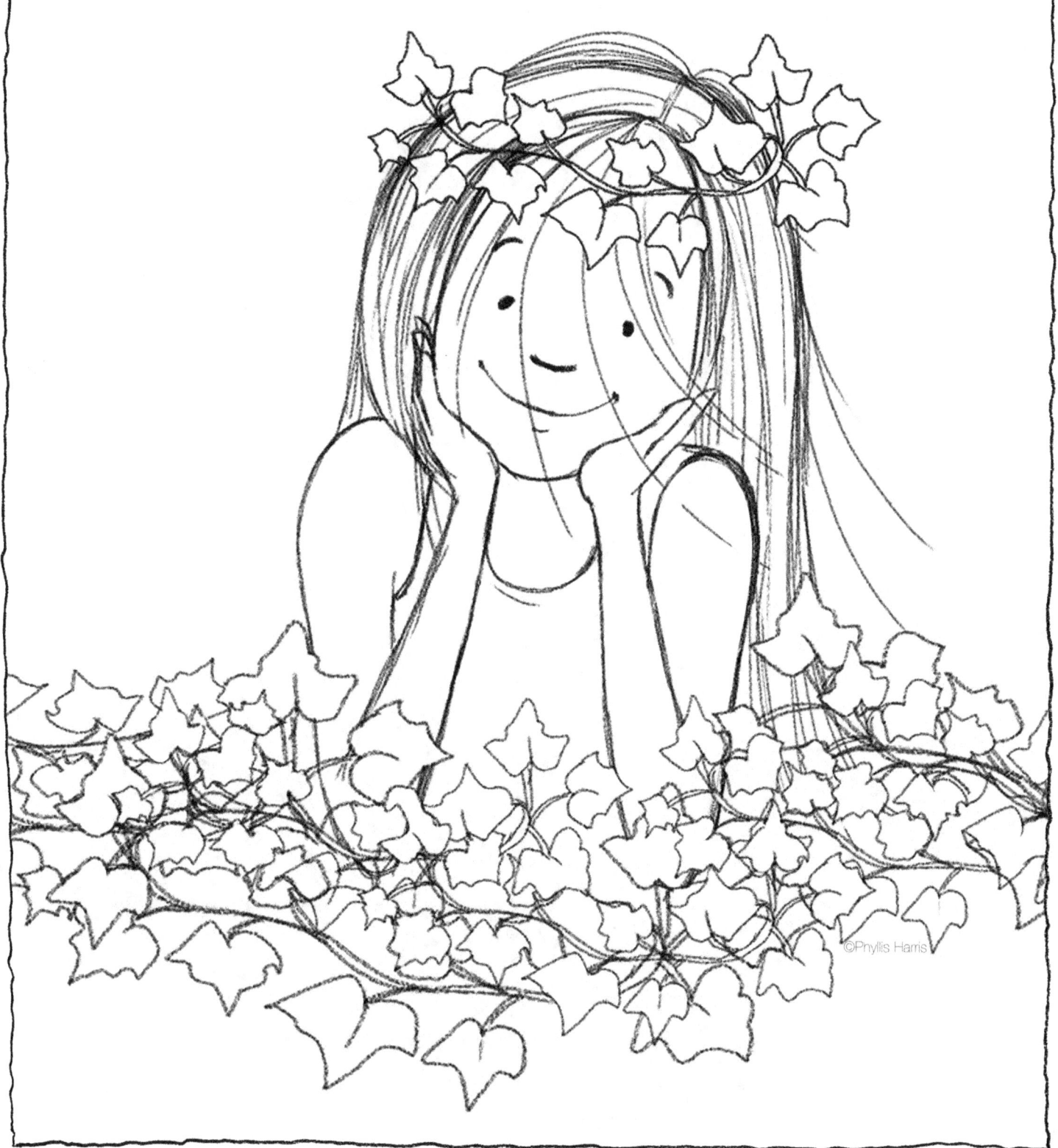

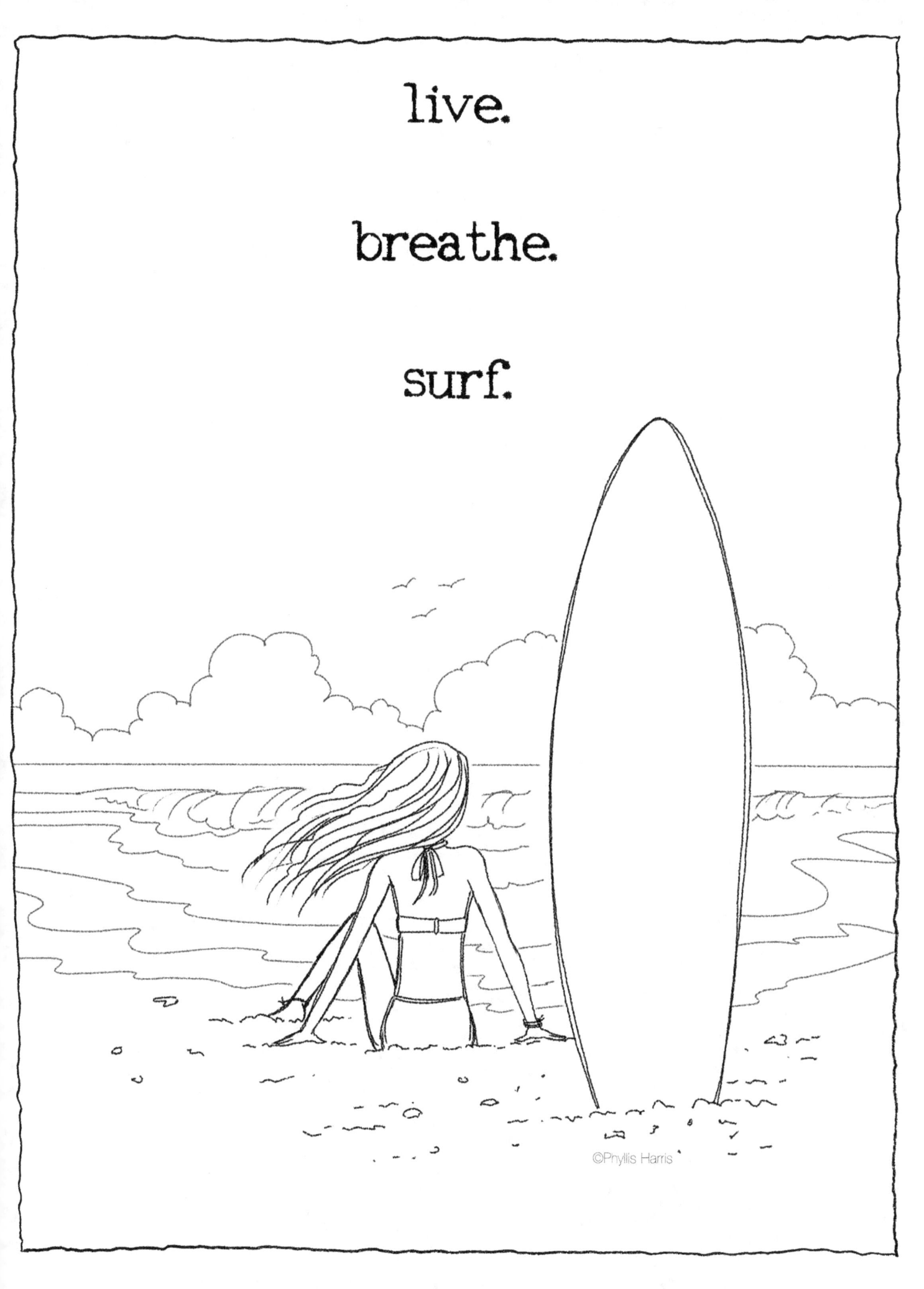

You rule over the majestic sea;

when its waves surge, you calm them.

Psalm 89:9

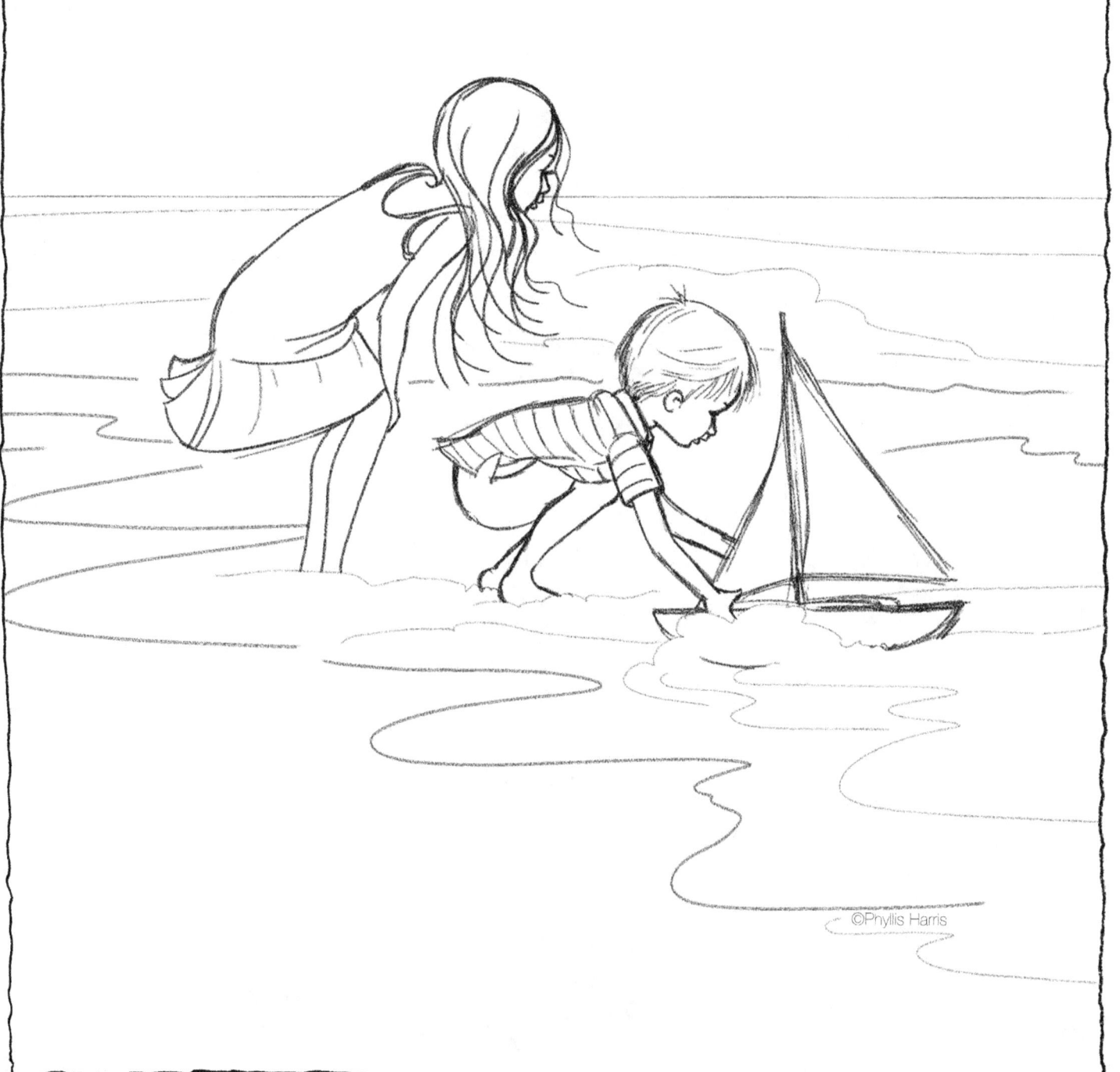

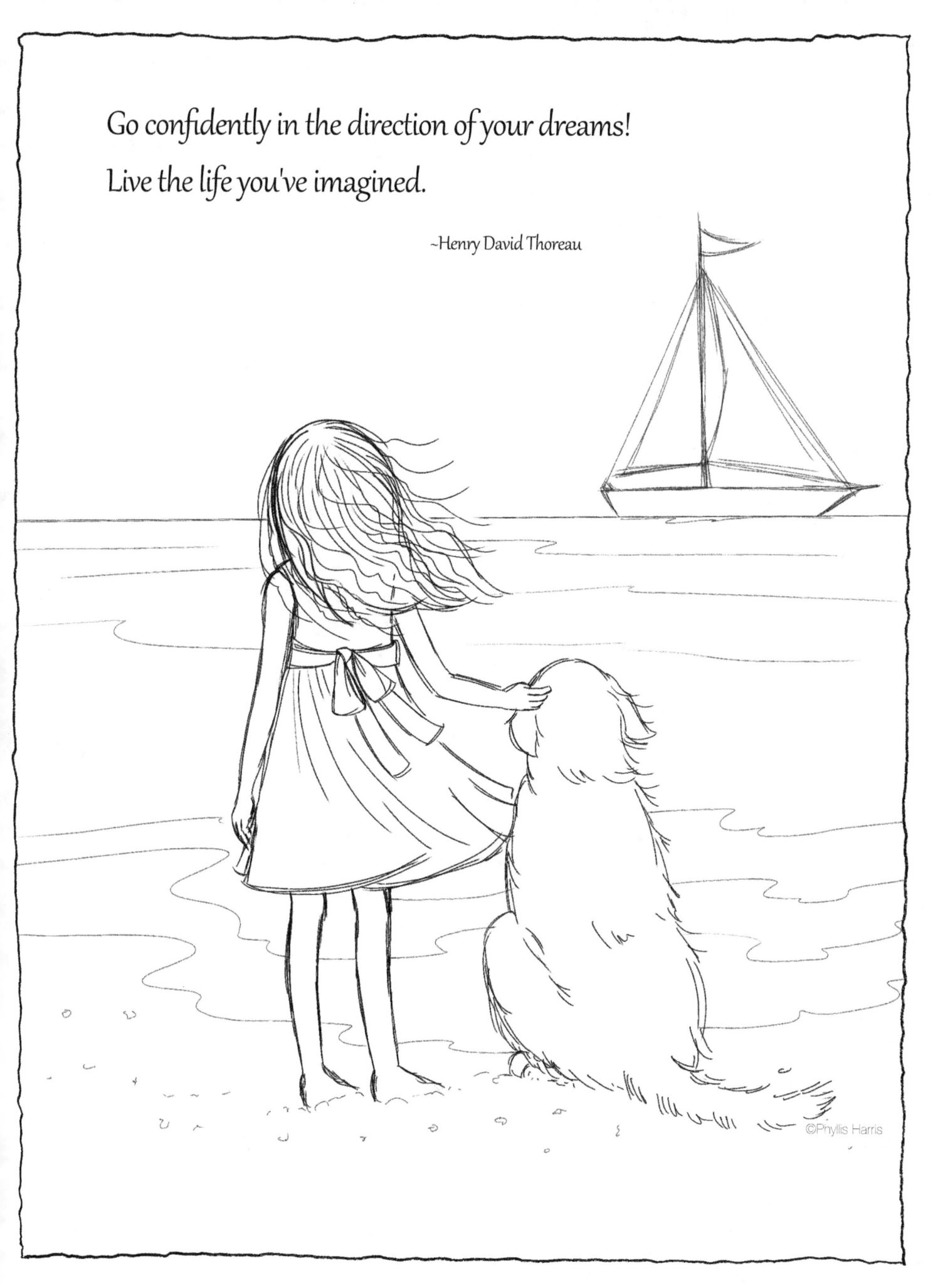

Go confidently in the direction of your dreams!

Live the life you've imagined.

~Henry David Thoreau

©Phyllis Harris

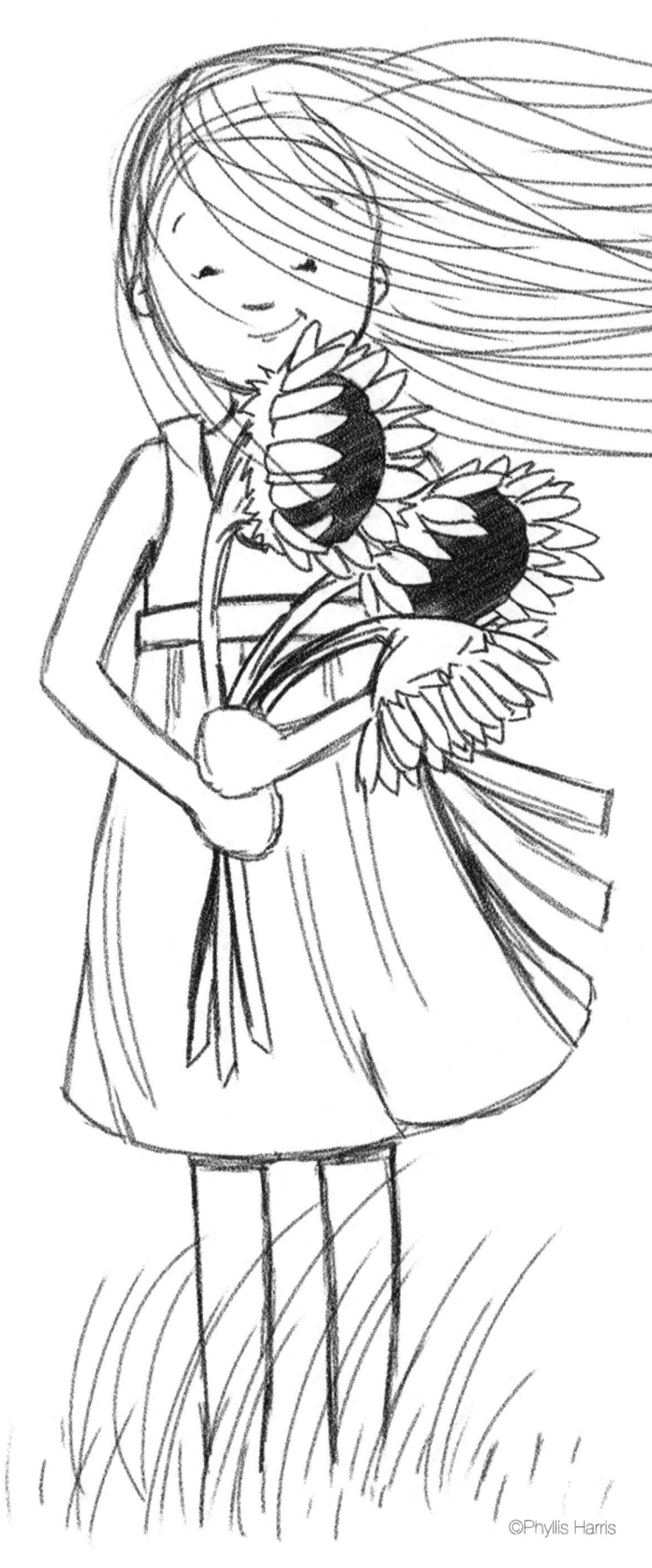

Keep your
face to the
sunshine
and you
cannot see
a shadow.

~Helen Keller

©Phyllis Harris

i knew i loved you before i met you...

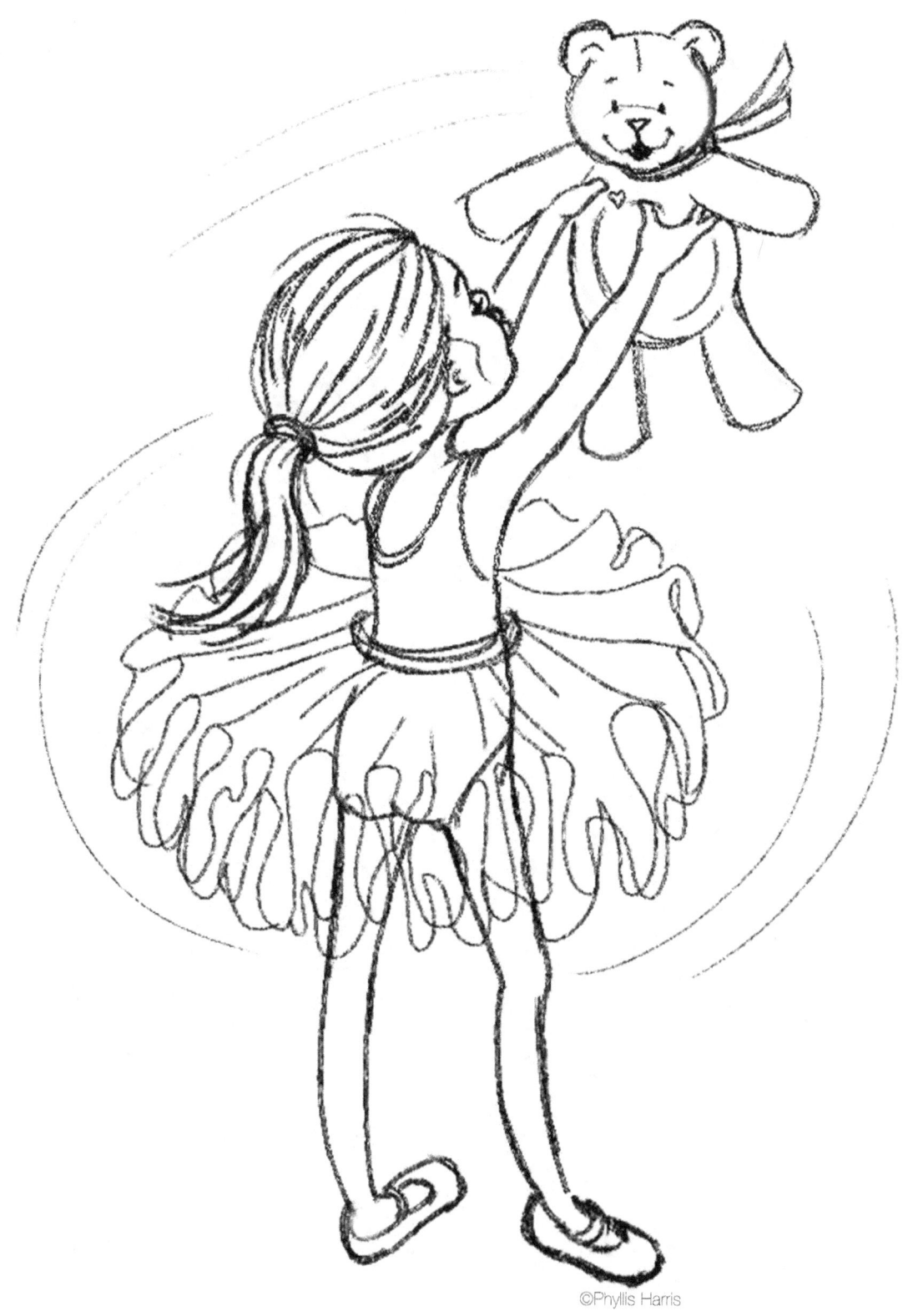

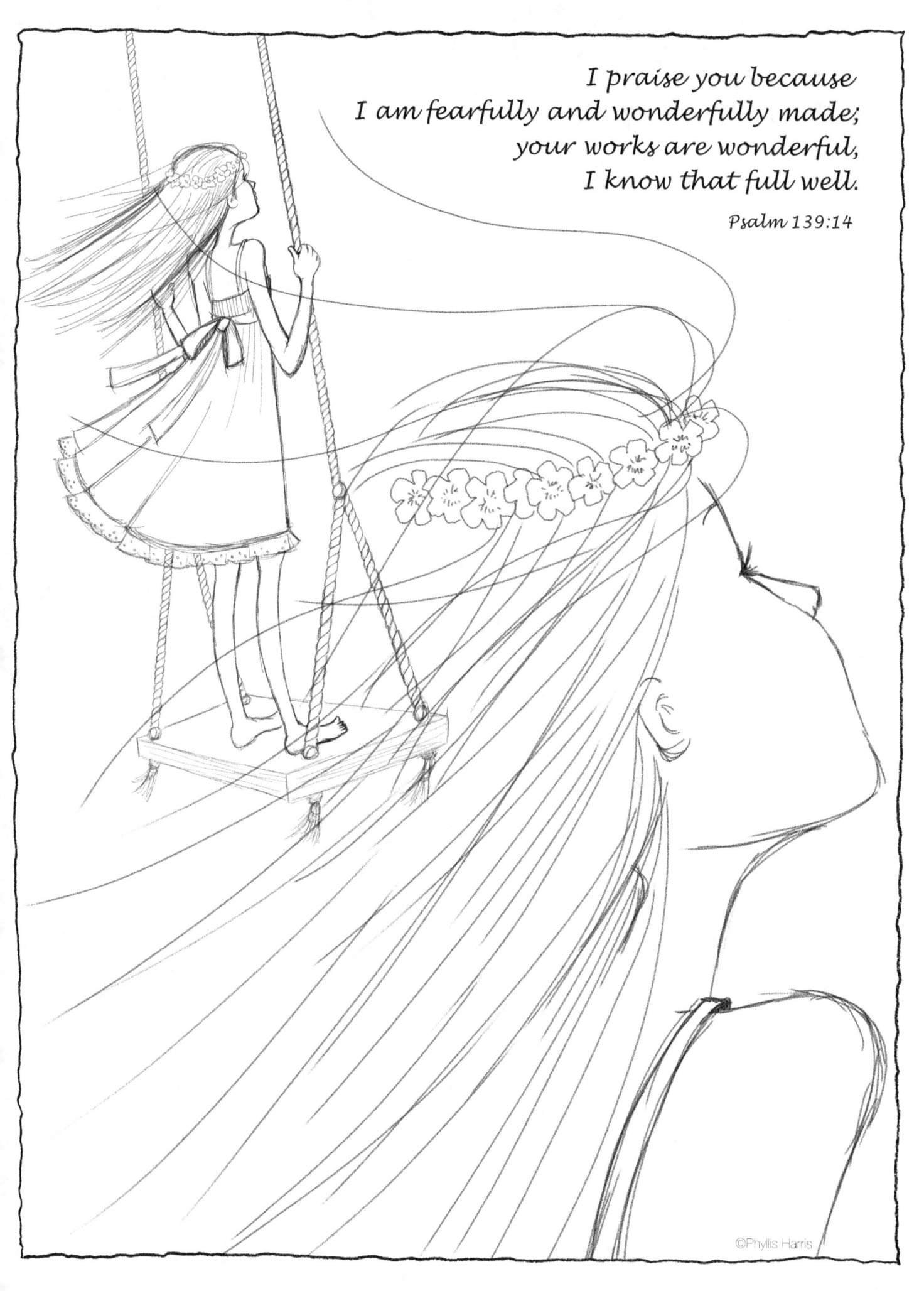

Be still
and know that I am God.

Psalm 46:10

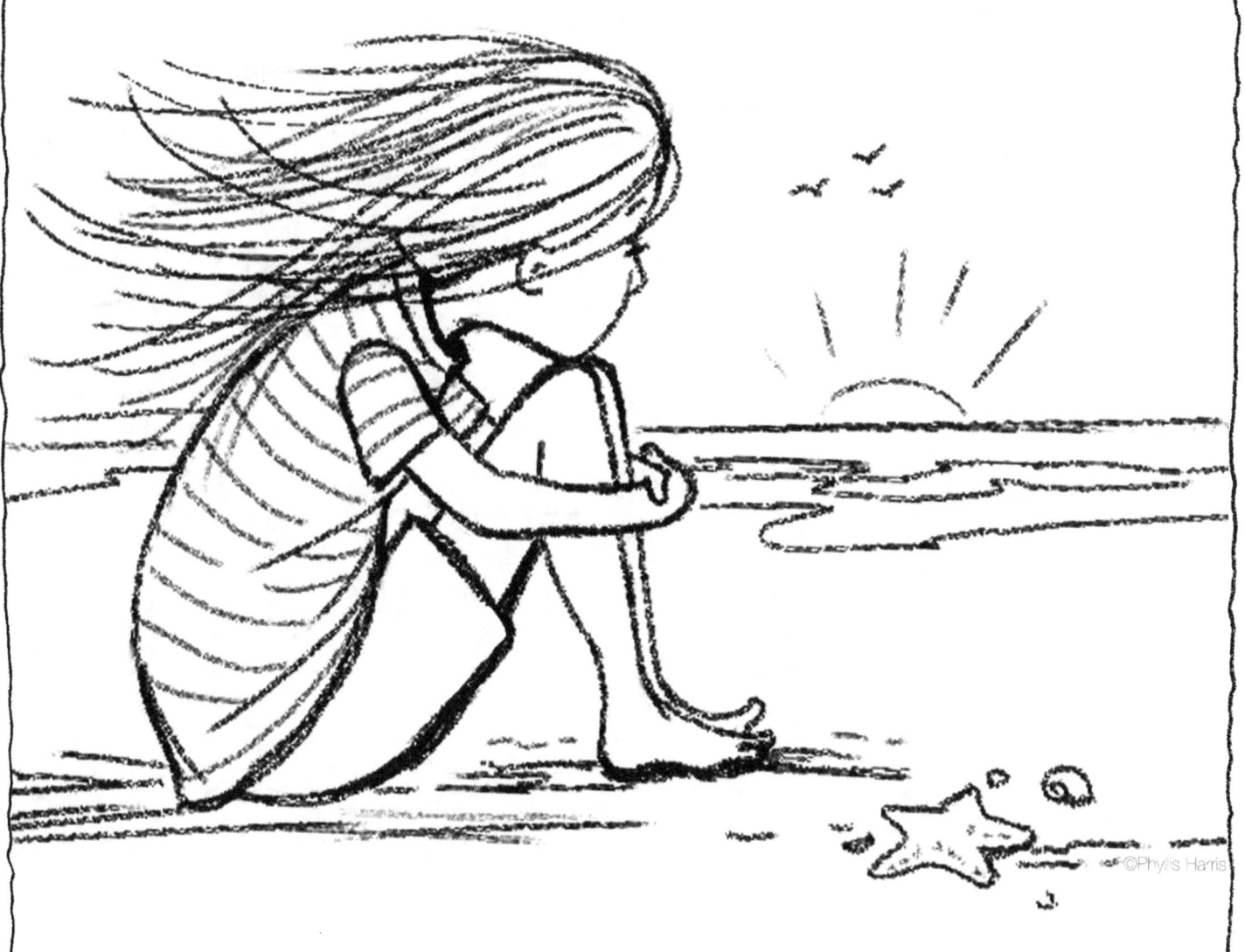

Lift up your eyes on high, and
behold who hath created these things

Isaiah 40:26

Most folks are as happy
as they make up their minds to be.

Abraham Lincoln

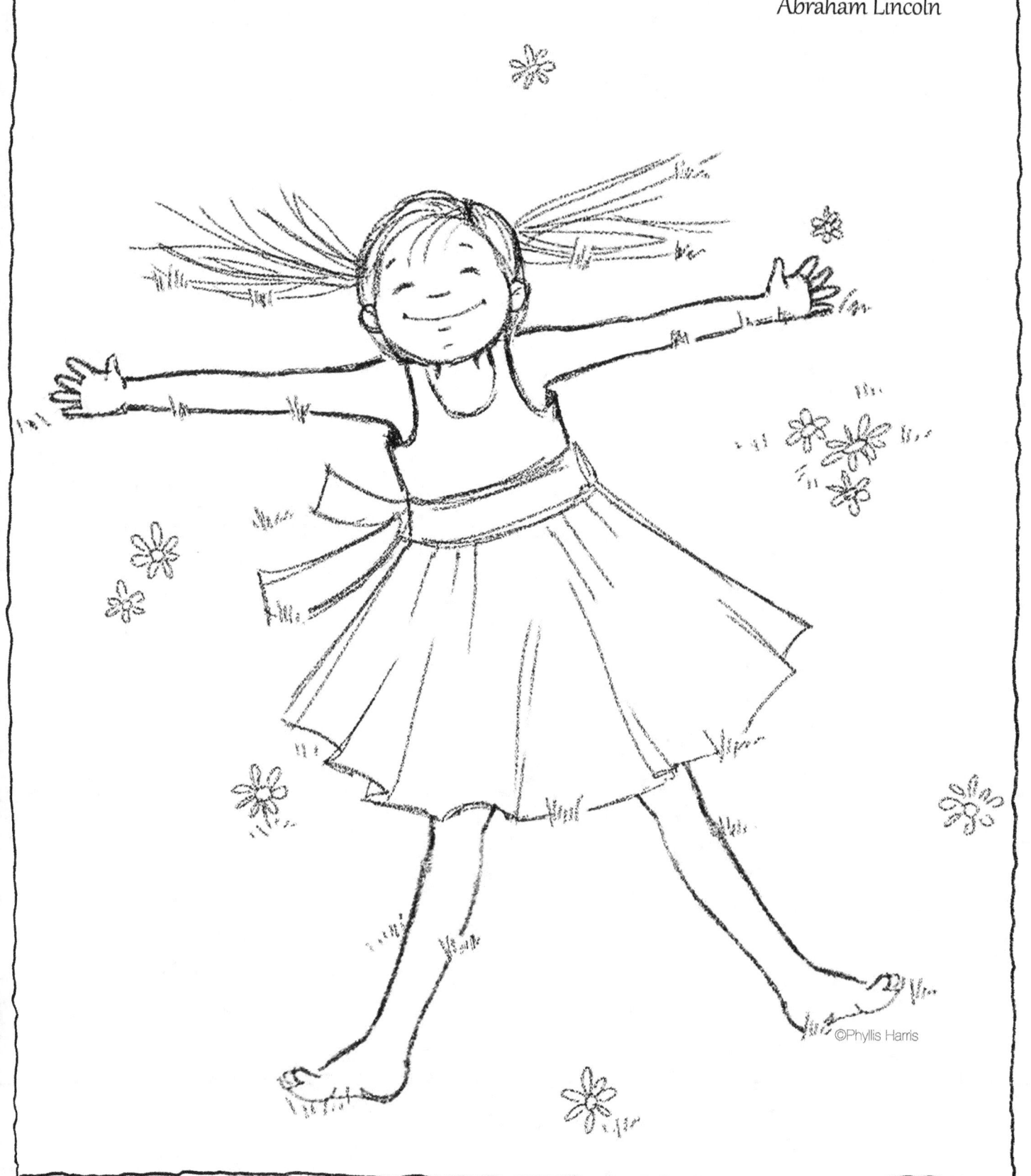

Behold,
I make all things new.

Revelation 21:5

©Phylis Harris

Whatever you are, be a good one.

Abraham Lincoln

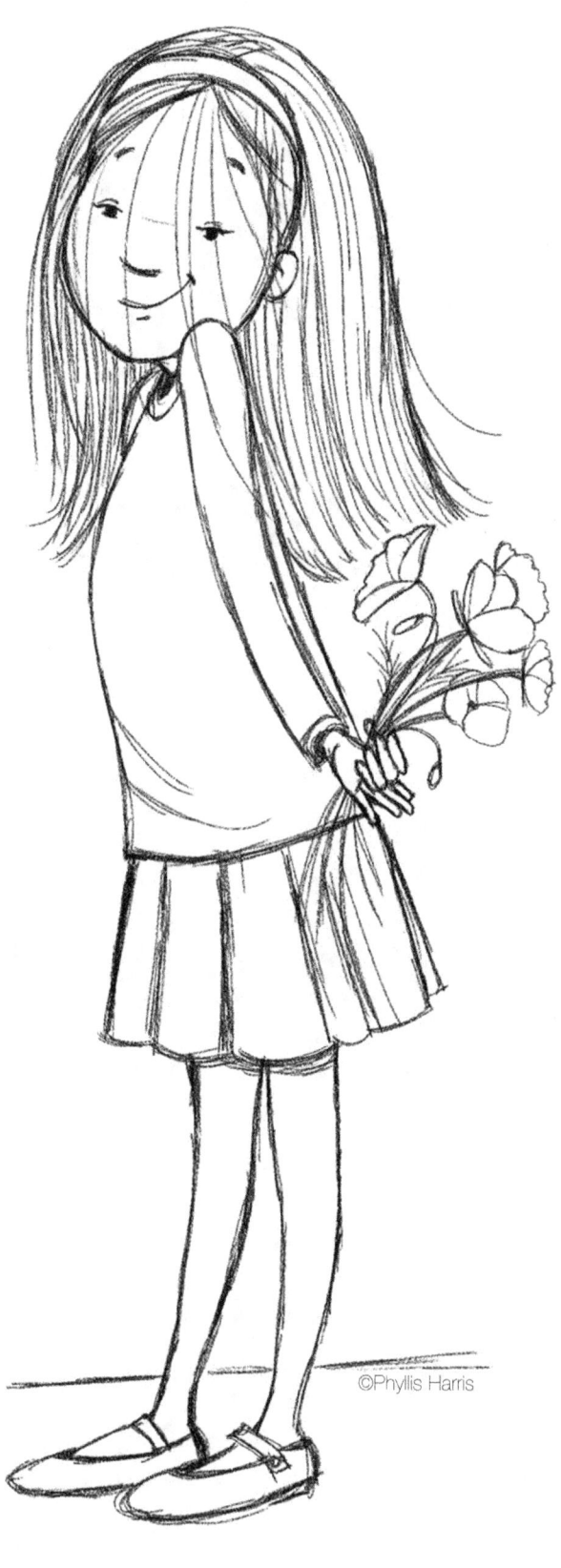

This is the day that the Lord has made;
I will rejoice and be glad in it.

Psalm 118:24

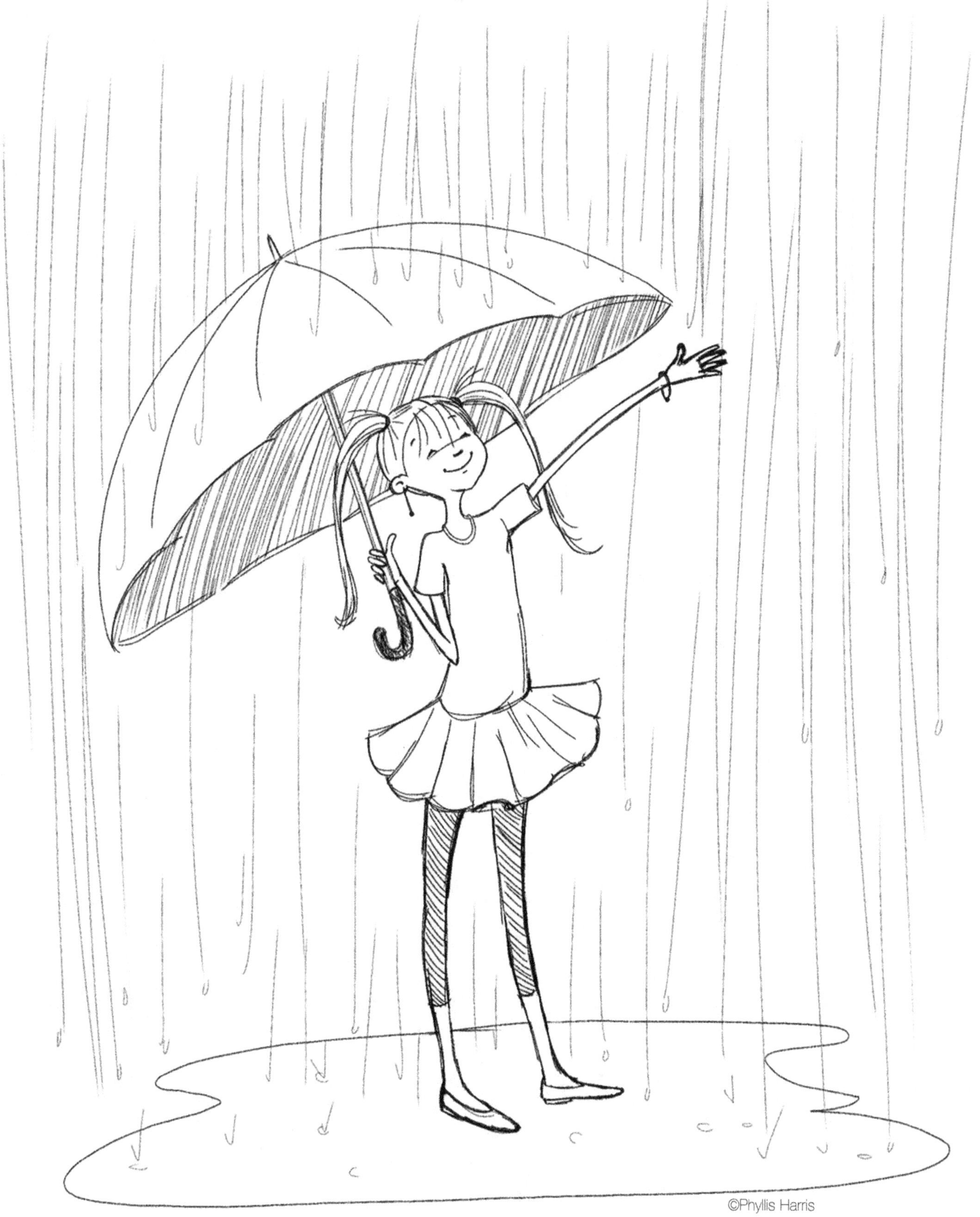

There are miracles all around us.

We only have to open our eyes to see them.

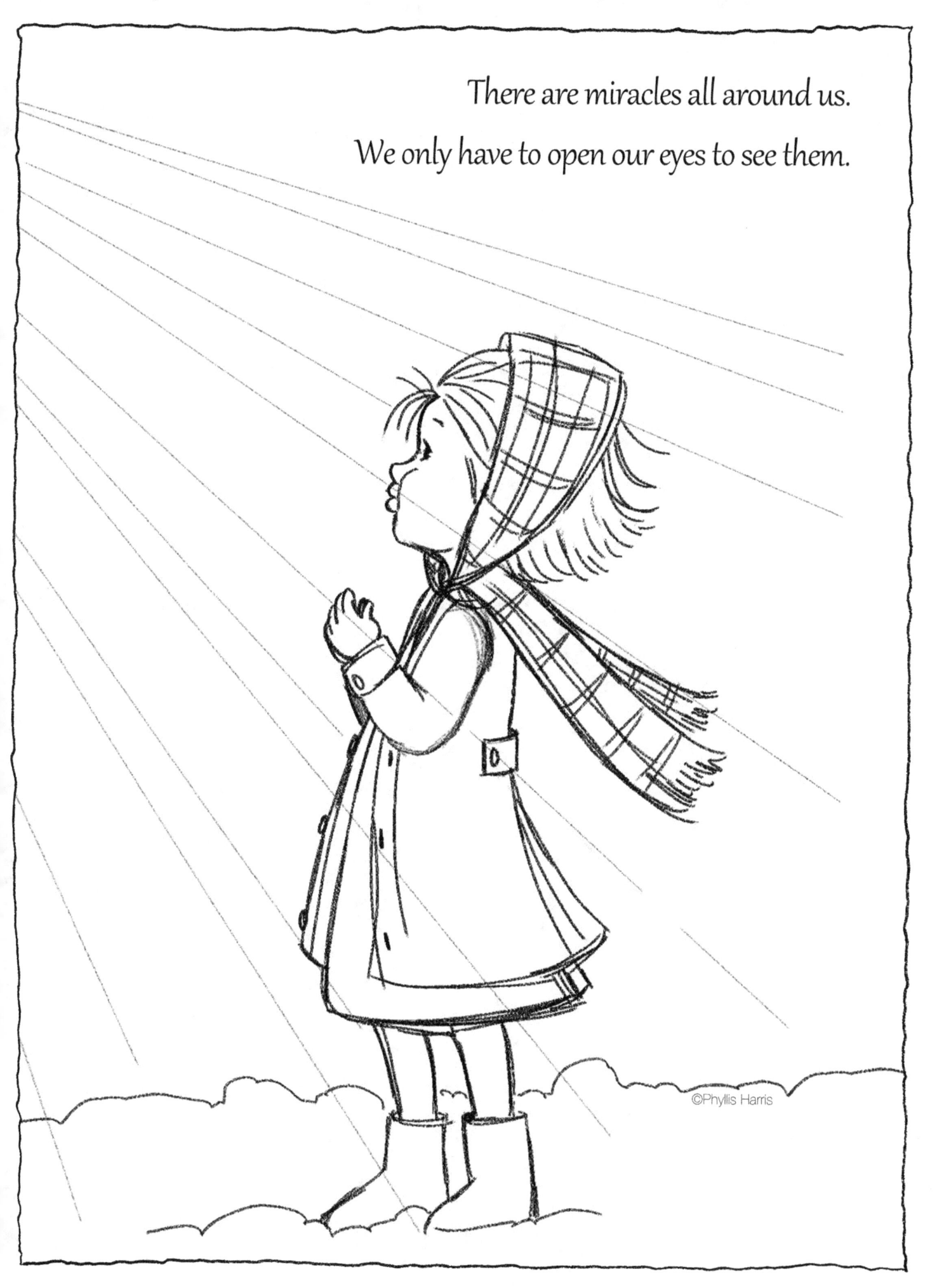

GOD MADE
THE HORSE
FROM THE
BREATH OF
THE WIND,
THE BEAUTY OF
THE EARTH,
AND THE SOUL
OF AN ANGEL.
~UNKNOWN

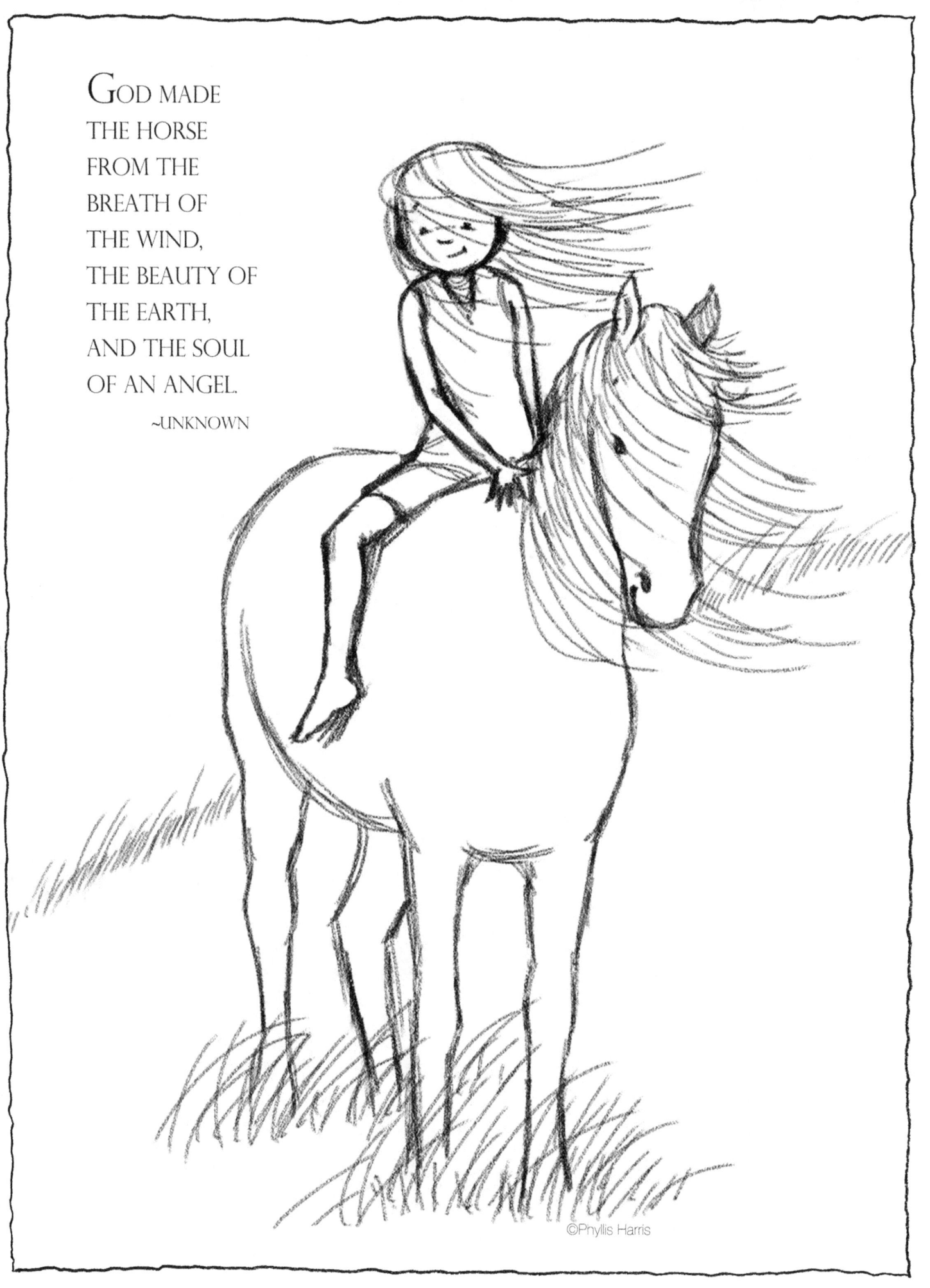

©Phyllis Harris

The best present is
the gift of
you.

©Phyllis Harris

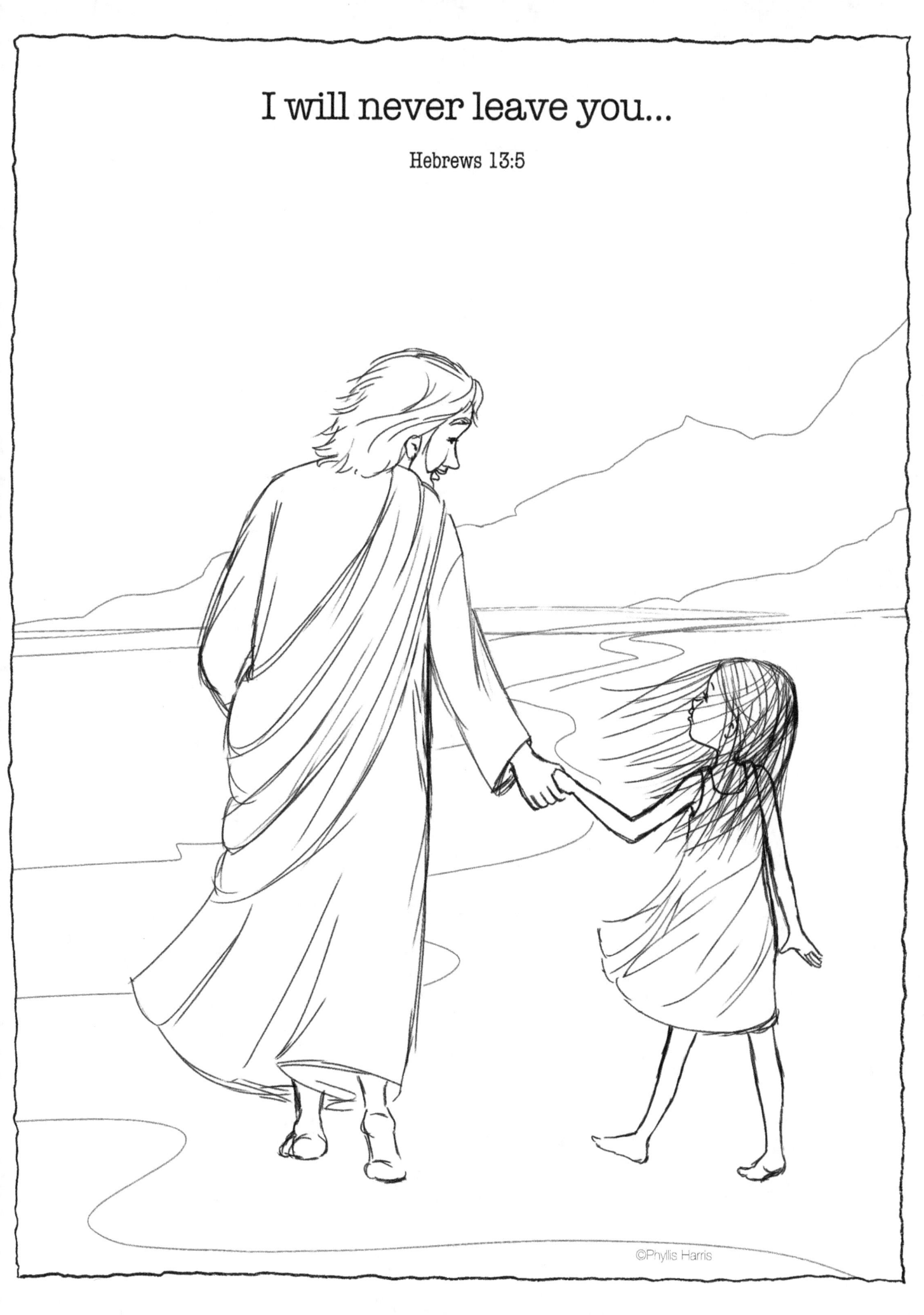

I will never leave you...

Hebrews 13:5

©Phyllis Harris

A teacher takes a hand,
opens a mind,
and touches a heart.

~Author Unknown

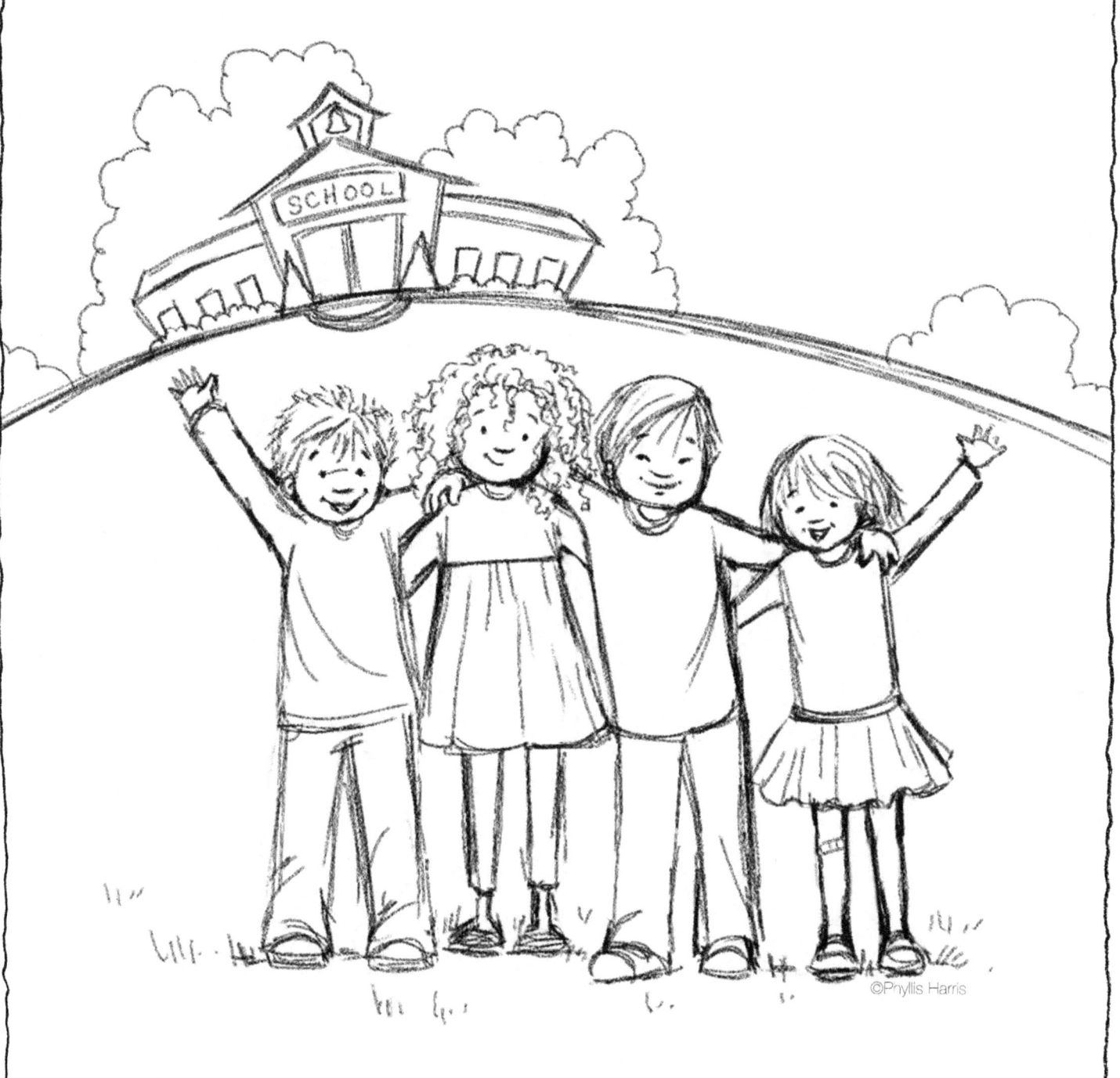

It's wonderful to climb
the liquid mountains
of the sky.
Behind me and
before me is God
and I have no fears.

-Helen Keller

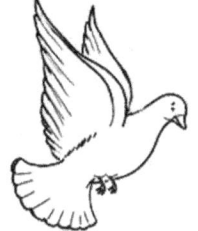

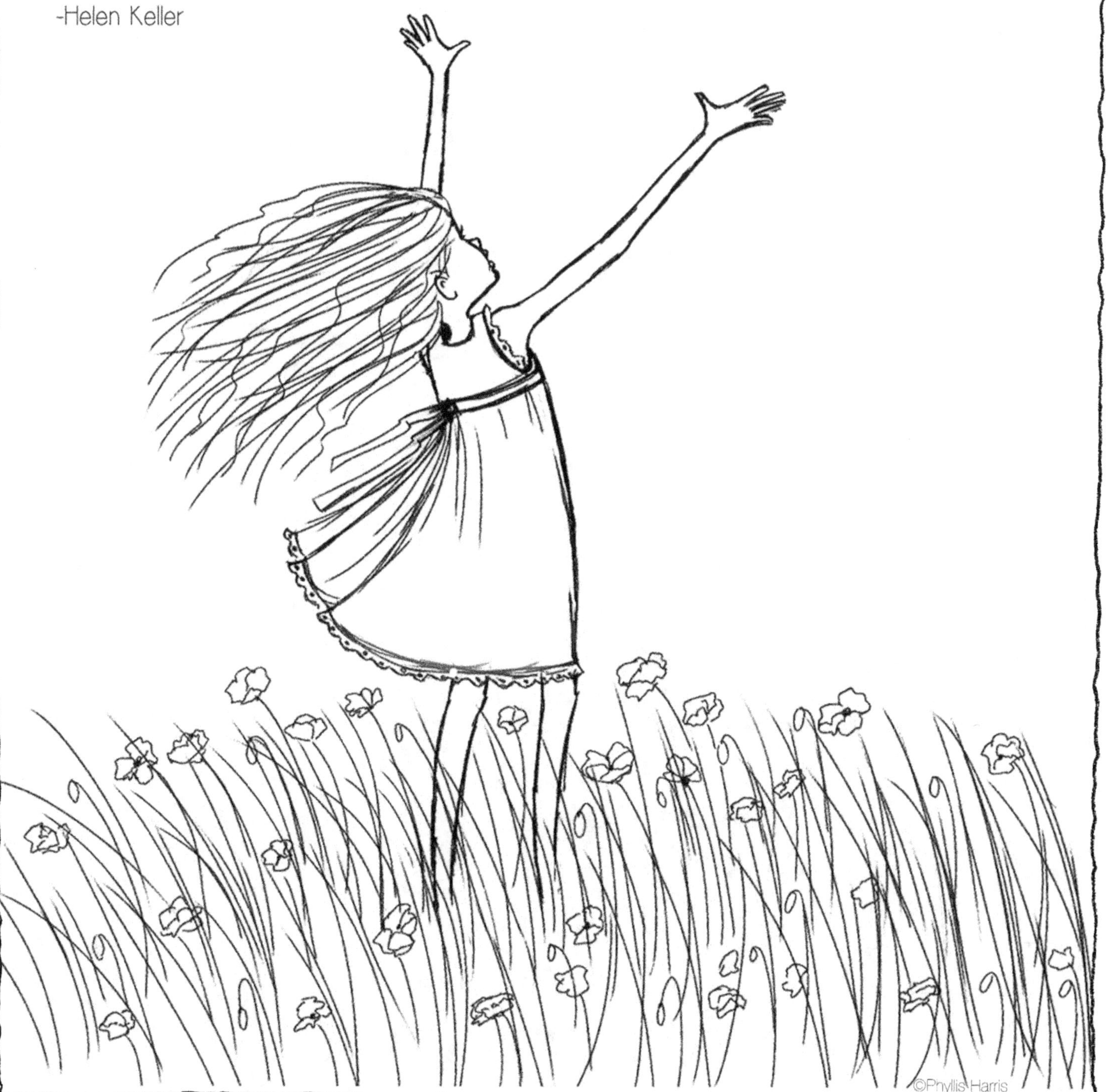

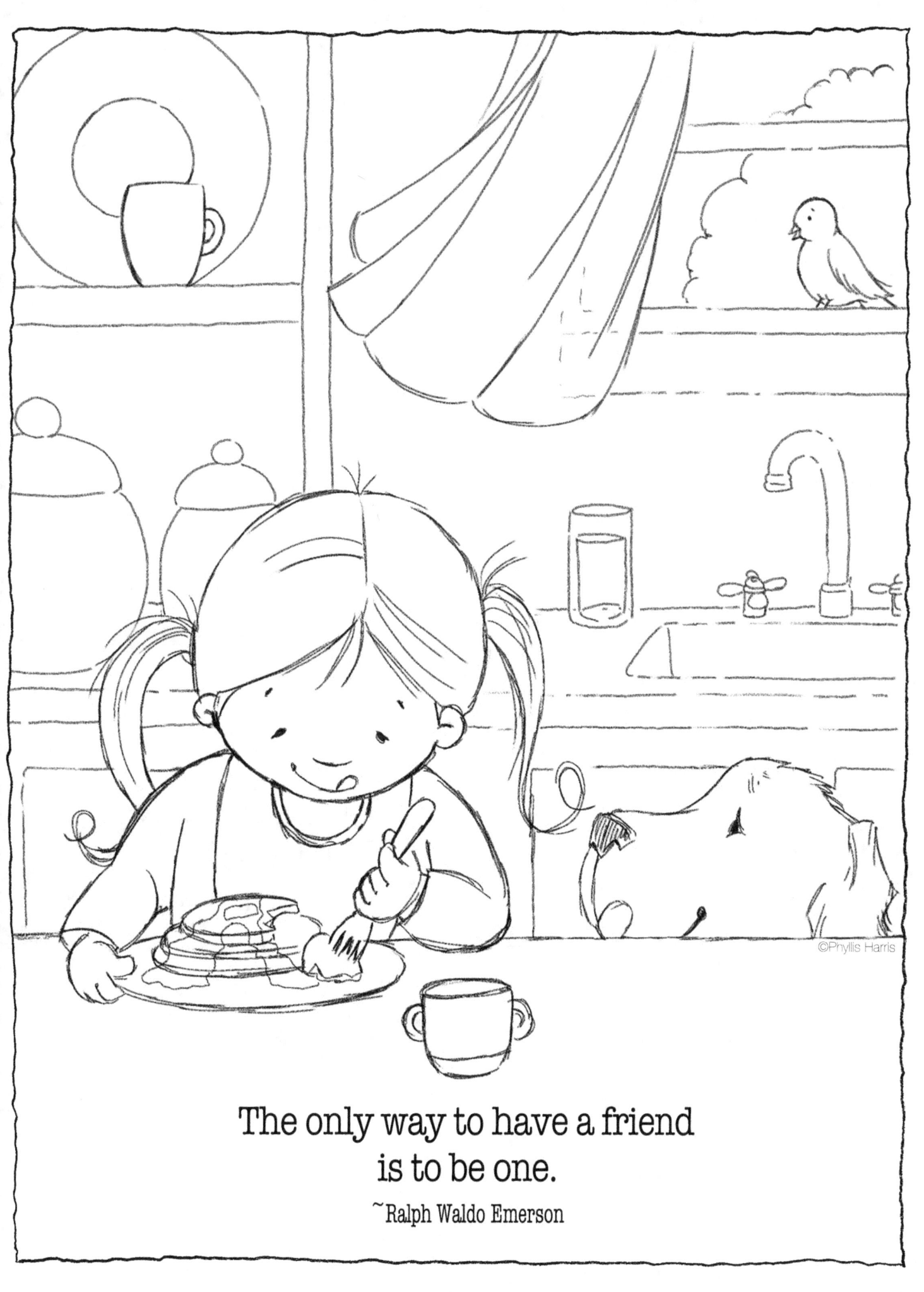

The only way to have a friend
is to be one.

~Ralph Waldo Emerson

Never lose your sense of wonder.

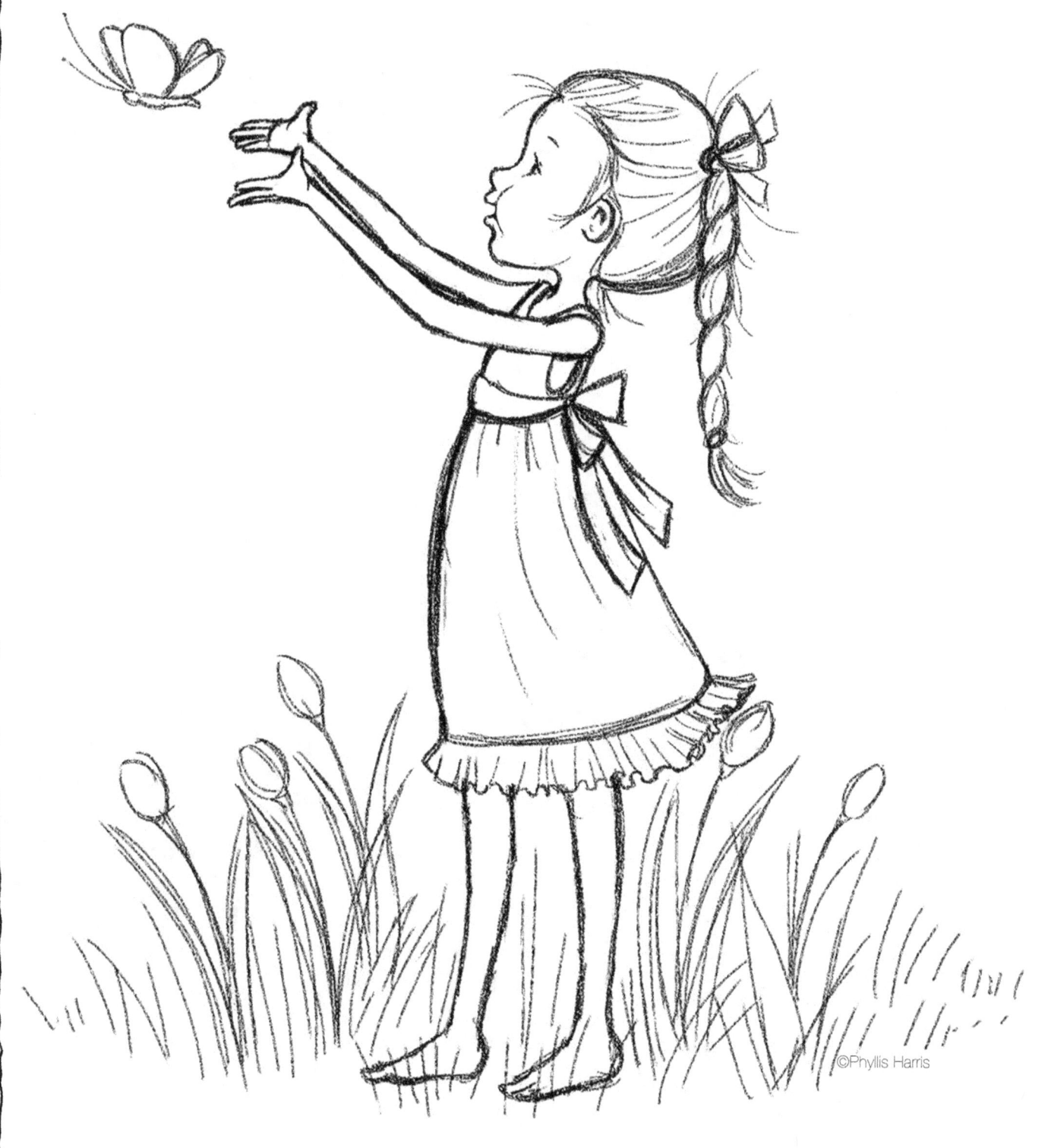

A friend loveth at all times...

Proverbs 17:17

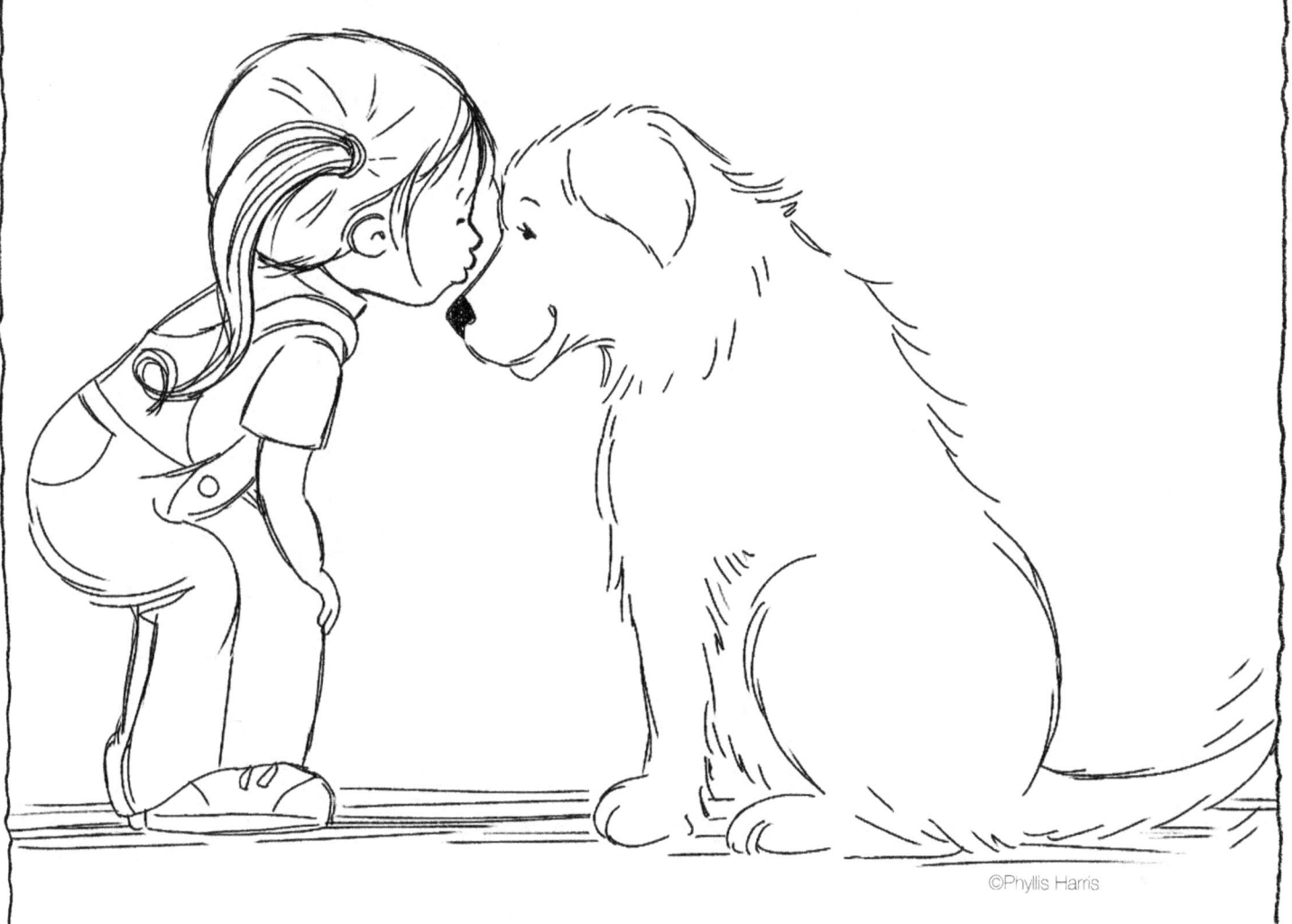

Every moment of light and **dark** is a miracle.
~Walt Whitman

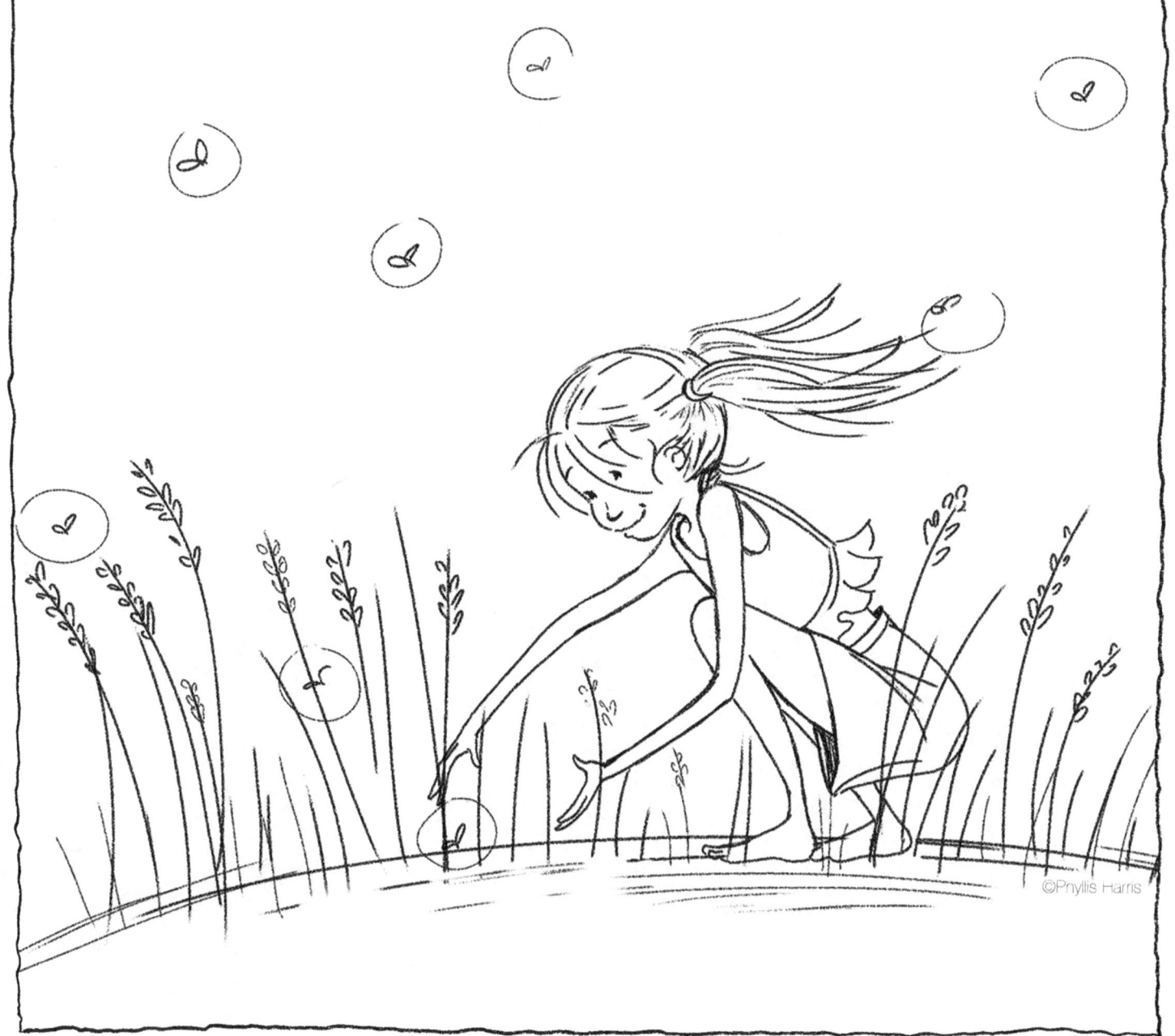

Blessed are the peacemakers,
for they will be called children of God.

Matthew 5 :9

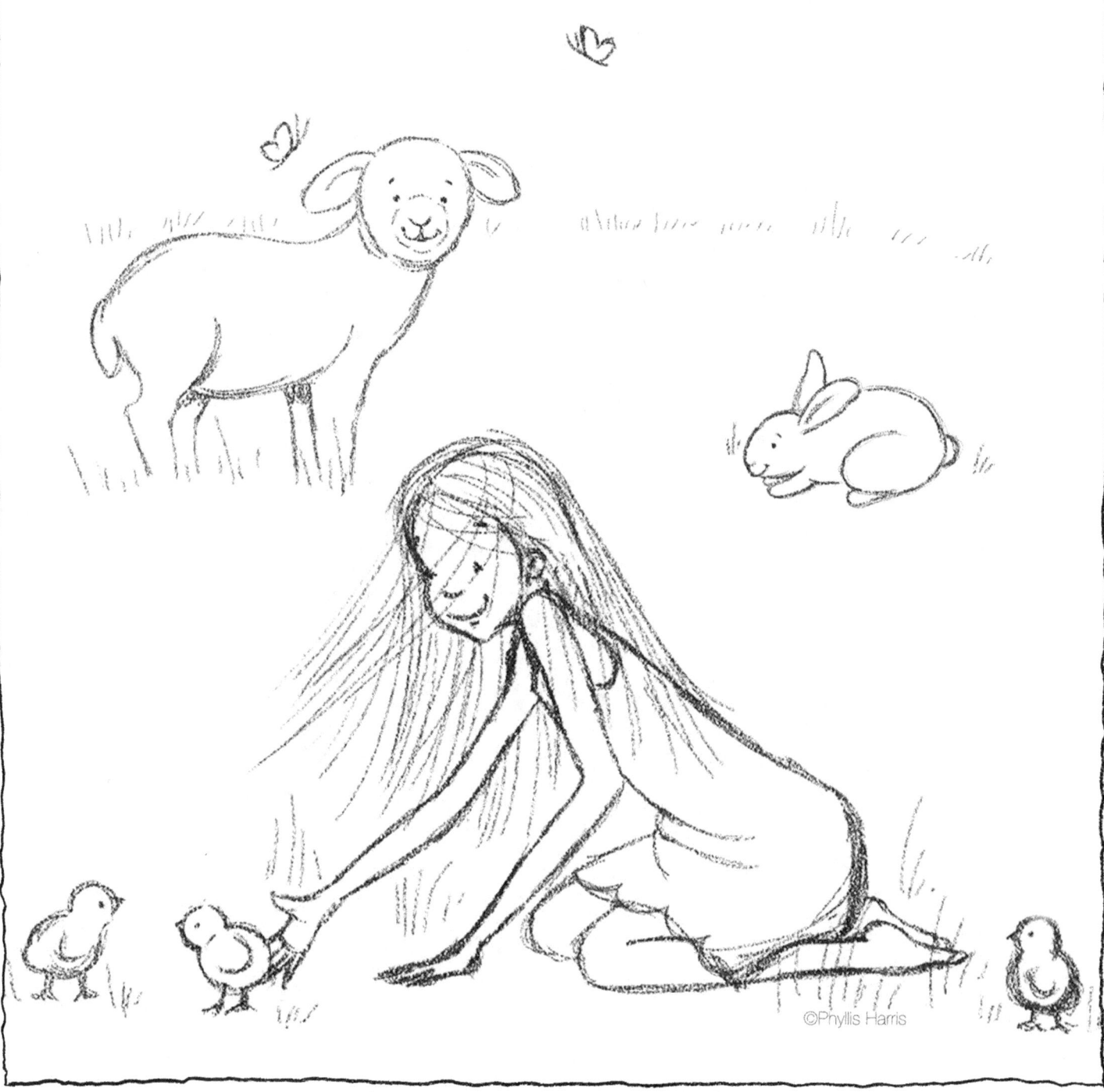

Be strong and *courageous.*
Do not be afraid;
do not be discouraged,
for the *Lord* your *God*
will be with *you*
wherever you go.

Joshua 1:9

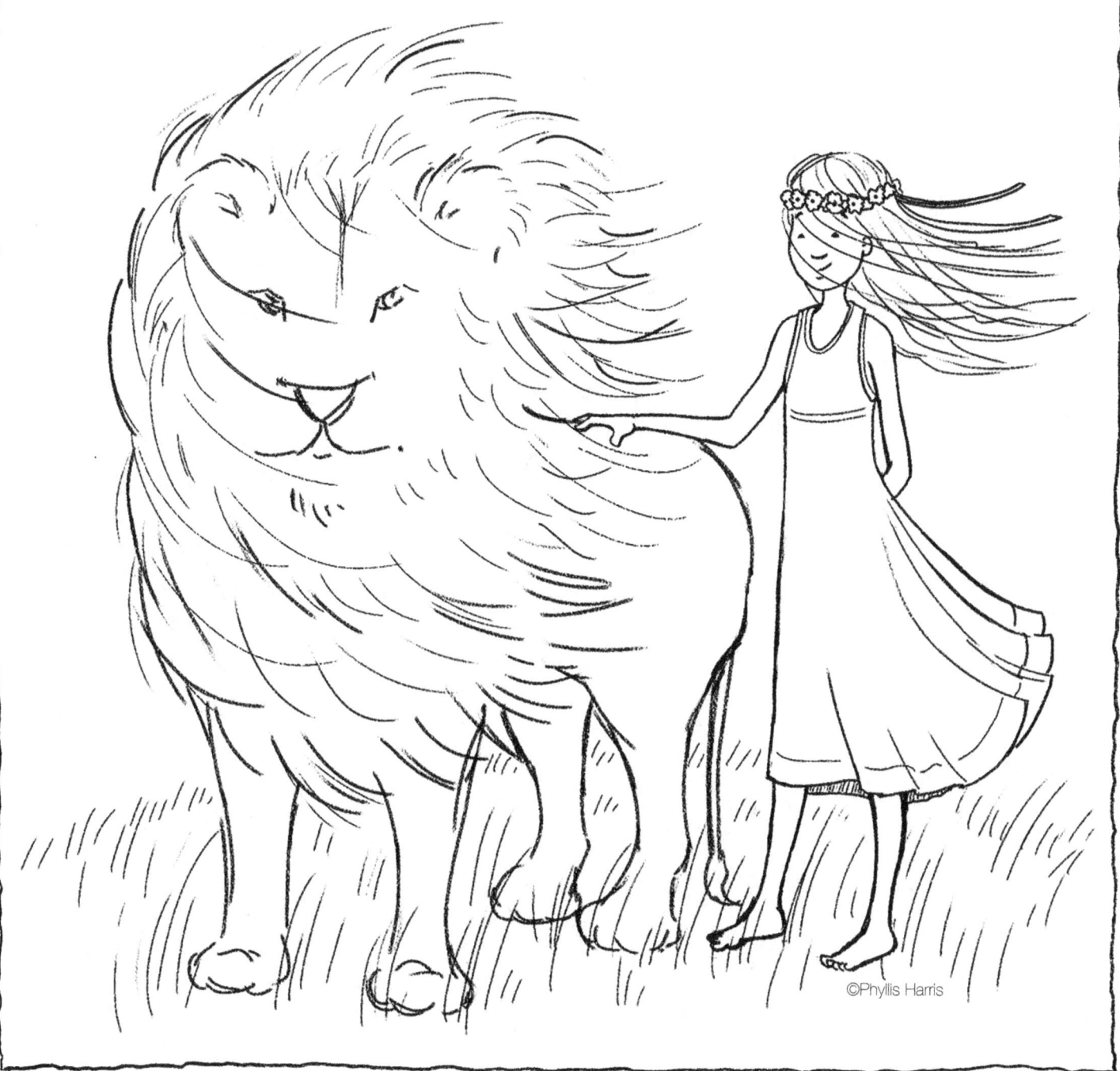

The only way to have a friend
is to be one. ~Ralph Waldo Emerson

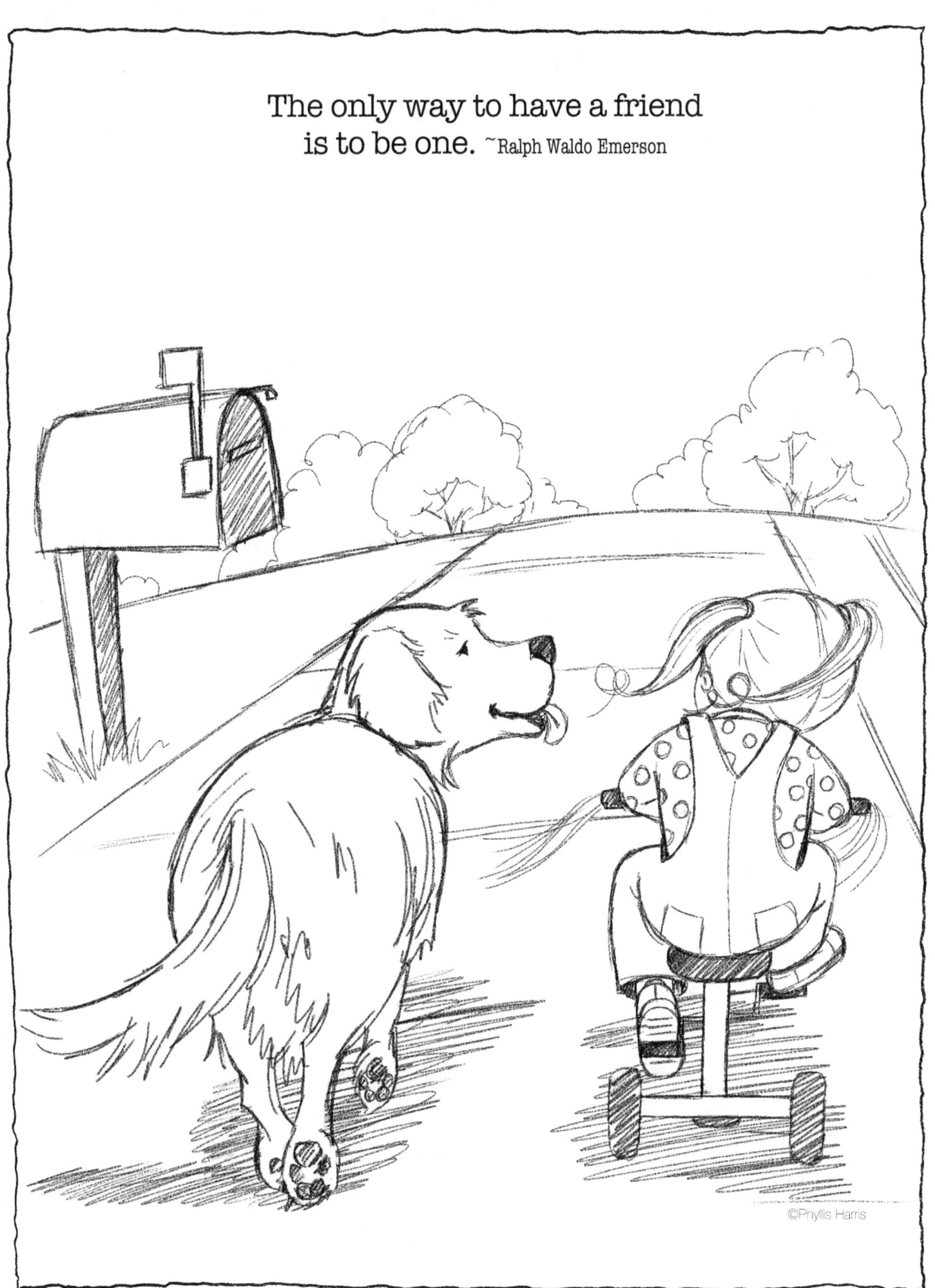